JOHANNA BURKHARD
FAST&EASY
COOKING

JOHANNA BURKHARD

FAST&EASY
COOKING

Robert ROSE

FAST & EASY COOKING

For complete cataloguing data, see page 6.

DESIGN AND PAGE COMPOSITION:	MATTHEWS COMMUNICATIONS DESIGN
PHOTOGRAPHY:	MARK T. SHAPIRO
ART DIRECTION/FOOD PHOTOGRAPHY:	SHARON MATTHEWS
FOOD STYLIST:	KATE BUSH
PROP STYLIST:	MIRIAM GEE
MANAGING EDITOR:	PETER MATTHEWS
INDEXER:	BARBARA SCHON
COLOR SCANS & FILM:	POINTONE GRAPHICS

Cover photo: ORANGE-BASIL CHICKEN STIR-FRY *(PAGE 99)*

Distributed in the U.S. by:
Firefly Books (U.S.) Inc.
P.O. Box 1338
Ellicott Station
Buffalo, NY 14205

Distributed in Canada by:
Stoddart Publishing Co. Ltd.
34 Lesmill Road
North York, Ontario
M3B 2T6

ORDER LINES
Tel: (416) 499-8412
Fax: (416) 499-8313

ORDER LINES
Tel: (416) 213-1919
Fax: (416) 213-1917

Published by: Robert Rose Inc. • 156 Duncan Mill Road, Suite 12
Toronto, Ontario, Canada M3B 2N2   Tel: (416) 449-3535

Printed in Canada

1234567 BP 01 00 99 98

CONTENTS

Canadian Cataloguing in Publication Data

Burkhard, Johanna
 Fast & easy cooking

Includes index.
ISBN 1-896503-81-0

1. Quick and easy cookery. I. Title. II. Title: Fast and easy cooking.

TX833.5.B874 1998   641.5'55   C98-931593-2

PHOTO PROP CREDIT

The author and publisher wish to express their appreciation to the following supplier of props used in the food photography appearing in this book:

PIER 1IMPORTS, TORONTO DISHES, ACCESSORIES, CUTLERY, LINENS

To my children
– Nicole and Patrick –
my joy and inspiration

Cooking is never just a solo effort – it's a communal affair. So I'd like to express my appreciation to the many people who have lent a hand or stirred a pot in creating this book.

Linda Kay, for her loyal friendship and help in editing this book.

My kitchen assistant, Melanie Ohlsson, for her expert help testing, tasting and evaluating my recipes.

My publisher, Bob Dees, for his dedication to the project and savvy marketing skills. Also to Denise Amram and Lori Bartholomew of Robert Rose Inc., for their work in selling the book; and to publicist Dianne Hargrave for her PR skills.

The creative team who makes the process go so smoothly: Matthews Communications Design, including Peter and Sharon Matthews, Tina Edan and Elaine Thompson; food stylist Kate Bush; and photographer Mark Shapiro.

My thanks to Norene Gilletz for her comprehensive nutritional analysis of the recipes.

Thanks go to *The Gazette* newspaper, *Canadian Living*, *Elm Street* and *Homemaker's* magazines, where some of these recipes may have appeared before.

Heartfelt thanks to my mother, Rica Vanderloo; my sisters, Maria Salmon and Willie Adema; as well as my family and friends for their continued support and encouragement.

My warmest thanks go to my family for sharing my passion for good food: my daughter Nicole, an enthusiastic vegetarian cook who is a great help shopping and testing recipes; my son Patrick, who is showing promise in the kitchen; and my husband Hans, who is always so supportive and always there for me.

Finally, I am delighted that, as with my *Comfort Food Cookbook*, this book is affiliated with The Children's Miracle Network, which is dedicated to raising funds for children's hospitals and foundations across North America.

Children's Miracle Network®

An Appreciation

The Children's Miracle Network (CMN) is an international non-profit organization dedicated to raising funds and awareness for children's hospitals and foundations.

Since our inception in 1983, over $1 billion has been raised for the cause. Our yearly efforts culminate in a television special which airs across North America in early June. This broadcast profiles many of the children who have been treated at children's hospitals and health centres across the country and focuses on the tenacity and courage of these young people. It also serves to educate the public on medical developments, research advances and how fund-raising dollars are spent.

The cornerstone of CMN's success is that **every cent raised locally stays right in the community where it was raised** to benefit Canadian children being treated by our member hospitals and health centres.

Children like Brandon, who was born with a rare genetic disorder called Apert Syndrome. This disorder caused the bones of Brandon's head, hands and feet to fuse together before birth. Three surgeries before the age of 2 – and more to come – have not daunted Brandon, who faces each recovery with a brave and cheerful attitude. He's an inspiration to all who meet him – especially when he talks about becoming a firefighter just like his Grandpa when he grows up!

The research, technology and equipment associated with Brandon's procedures – as well as the ongoing work in prevention and treatment of childhood diseases, birth defects and life-threatening accidents and illnesses – are the reason CMN exists.

Funds raised through CMN programs are used by the hospitals and health centres to ensure that a high level of specialized care is available to our children when they need it and to continue outreach, wellness and safety programs to keep children healthy and happy in their communities.

On behalf of all the 2 million children treated by our Canadian member hospitals each year, we extend a sincere thank you to Johanna Burkhard for her generosity in dedicating a portion of the sale of this book to CMN.

Sincerely,

Stephanie Melemis

VICE-PRESIDENT, CANADA
CHILDREN'S MIRACLE NETWORK

Introduction

What's for dinner? The question is on our minds as we stampede home at rush hour. Cooking today is as much about the demands on our time as about what we're serving for dinner.

We're all trying to balance jobs with a busy family life. And like most people, I don't have much time to spend in the kitchen when I arrive home. Dinner often plays second fiddle to juggling work schedules, home-work and a host of activities that demand our time. Yet suppers need to be appetizing and nutritious.

With our hectic schedules and frantic pace, it's almost impossible to make a meal from scratch every night. Who has the time anymore?

If you're daunted by the daily task of getting supper on the table, *Fast & Easy Cooking* offers plenty of meal-time options. In about the same time that it takes to order a pizza and have it delivered, you can have a delicious dinner on the table.

How? Simply by adopting time-saving strategies to make your kitchen time more manageable. Here are some of the strategies that work for me.

Planning a weekly menu sounds like a good idea, but for me (and for most people) they're impractical – after all, family schedules change almost daily. It also means having to spend time on yet another house-hold chore. So I made a compromise.

Now I simplify my planning by limiting to 15 minutes a week the time I devote to designing a rough meal plan and drafting a shopping list. Plus, I only plan for 4 to 5 dinners because it's not always easy to predict whether I will be cooking every night of the week. I always plan a pasta dish, a chicken or fish dish, a recipe that I can double, plus something new – often a vegetarian recipe.

It's a formula that works for me, but you can create your own. I stick the list on the fridge and refer to it

daily. I revise it if our family schedule changes as the week goes on.

Not only does this method save me time, it also saves me money because I don't make unnecessary trips to the supermarket or rely on take-out or fast-food meals.

I've also redefined the traditional notion of what qualifies as "dinner." It needn't be a complicated meal. A hearty bowl of vegetable minestrone and good crusty bread or a turkey patty tucked in a pita pocket and topped with crunchy vegetable salsa count as dinner in my house. The dishes are satisfying and nourishing – and easy enough for my teenagers to cook.

Today's home cooks are looking for meals that are simple and reliable, yet reassuringly familiar. Still, it's easy to get in a rut when planning meals, with the result that you rely on only a handful of recipes. Break the habit of cooking the same dishes week after week. Plan on trying one new recipe each week. Get your family involved in the decision-making so that everyone's tastes are considered. There's no sense planning what you think your family wants for dinner only to find that you end up as a nightly short-order cook catering to everyone's whims.

My aim in writing this book is to help streamline the daily chore of getting dinner on the table. *Fast & Easy Cooking* offers a new strategy for getting a great dinner ready in a hurry. On the nights when I do have more time, I get a head start on another meal by chopping the vegetables or doubling the recipe I'm cooking that night and freezing it for another meal. For example, I'll cook the rice for tomorrow's **Speedy Beef and Vegetable Fried Rice** (page 70) or make a double batch of **Mini Veal Meat Loaves** (page 59) to freeze for another supper. As well, many of the recipes can be completed ahead and reheated to save valuable time.

This collection of recipes is geared to cooks who want tasty meals – fast. Many of these quick dishes are personal favorites that have become standards in my house. And since my daughter is a vegetarian, I've included plenty of easy grain, rice and pasta options, such as **Greek Rice and Spinach Bake** (page 130) and **All-in-One Pasta and Chickpea Ragout** (page

117), that are a breeze to make and appealing even to non-vegetarians.

Helpful hints to speed preparation accompany many of the recipes in this book. I have focused on dishes that require little stirring or attention, or those that can be simply done in a single pot or casserole for easy clean-up.

Many of the recipes rely on time-saving convenience products found in supermarkets. To help cope with the six-o'clock rush, I count on canned stock, pasta-ready tomato sauces, assorted canned beans (such as kidney and black beans), salsas, grated cheeses, the new assortment of frozen vegetables, prewashed salad greens and ready-cut vegetables. All of them come to the rescue and help me get dinner on the table in a jiffy.

As a bonus, many of these recipes meet the guidelines for healthy eating – with no more that 30 percent of calories coming from fat. Feeding your family healthy delicious meals in a flash is far easier than you think. So let's get started!

Don't feel compelled to revamp your whole cooking style, but picking up some of these tips will make life simpler in the kitchen.

HOW TO SAVE TIME SHOPPING

Before you go – get organized. How many times have you wandered the aisles of a supermarket ran-domly picking up familiar foods? This is a recipe for costly impulse buys. Getting organized before you go shopping will make your life easier in the kitchen and save you money.

Make a list. Decide what meals you are going to make. Scan your pantry and fridge and jot down missing staples. Add to that any other items called for in recipes. Organize your shopping list according to the supermarket layout, grouping food items such as fresh meats, dairy, produce and canned goods togeth-er, so you won't have to backtrack.

Go shopping at the right time. You're likely to pur-chase more groceries than you intended if you shop when you're hungry. Try also not to shop when you're

tired or not in the mood – shopping is a weekly necessity so make it as pleasant and enjoyable as possible.

Take advantage of time-saving products. Items such as pasta-ready tomato sauces, precut vegetables and shredded cheeses cost more but are worth the price when it comes to saving time in the kitchen.

Try warehouse and bulk shopping. Buying in bulk can save you money – and time. However, the cost savings can evaporate if the products aren't used at peak freshness. Be sure to plan more carefully when purchasing in bulk so you don't overbuy.

Make shopping a family event. Get your family involved in the kitchen – and in the shopping routine. Cooking is an important life skill that goes hand in hand with food selection and buying. Children, in particular, need to know how to make wise food choices.

10 STRATEGIES FOR SAVING TIME IN THE KITCHEN

1. Wash lettuce as soon as you get home from the supermarket. Fill a sink with cold water, swish the leaves around and scoop them out into a salad spinner to dry. Wrap lettuce in a clean, dry kitchen towel and place in a plastic bag or store right in the salad spinner in the fridge.

2. Peel a week's worth of onions. Store in a plastic bag in the fridge. (To avoid odors, I prefer not to chop the onions ahead.) Not only will you save time prepping onions for recipes, the cold temperature will help minimize tears when you chop them.

3. You can also keep handy bags of chopped onions and sweet or hot peppers in the freezer to add to soups, casseroles and stews. Freeze for up to 3 months.

4. Separate a head of garlic into cloves and remove skins. Place in covered container in fridge; use within a week.

5. Peel ginger and store in a glass jar filled with sherry in the fridge. Use the ginger-flavored sherry in recipes.

6. To get a head start on another meal, cook extras such as rice, pasta and potatoes. Pack in covered containers; label and date. Store in the fridge for up to 3 days.

7. Double a recipe, where indicated, and freeze for another meal. Use masking tape and a permanent marker to label and date all freezer foods. Take stock of the foods often so items will be used at peak quality.

8. Batch-cook on weekends so you can rely on the fridge or freezer for make-ahead meals.

9. Don't let forgotten leftovers in the fridge become costly throw-aways. Place in a covered container, label and date. Store on a designated shelf in the fridge so everyone in the family will know where to find them.

10. Take advantage of your microwave to shortcut recipes such as steaming vegetables for stir-frys, melting butter and chocolate, and making quick sauces.

7 WAYS TO STREAMLINE YOUR KITCHEN

1. Knick-knacks or non-essential appliances clutter a kitchen counter. Keep only essential cooking equipment such as a food processor and coffee maker handy on your counter. Keep less-used items in the cupboard within easy reach.

2. Get a jug or crock for wooden spoons, tongs and spatulas and keep on the counter next to the stove.

3. Organize your kitchen drawers to keep similar utensils and kitchen tools together – for example, paring knives with vegetable peelers.

4. The same goes for cooking equipment such as saucepans, mixing bowls and baking equipment stored in cupboards. Have equipment used on a regular basis in easy reach; store all others in the back of cupboard.

5. Place your cutting board next to the sink; this will allow you to wash produce easily. Place a bowl nearby to dispose of vegetable waste for outdoor composting or for the garbage bin.

6. Organize your pantry so you can find items easily – and quickly see what's missing when making a grocery list. Group canned and packaged goods such as pastas on the same shelf. Arrange bottled vinegars and oils together along with condiments like ketchup and sauces like soya sauce.

7. Make sure everyone in the family is familiar with the kitchen set-up so that when it's their turn to clean up or put groceries away, everything will be put in the right place.

5 EASY STEPS FOR PREPARING A RECIPE

1. Read the entire recipe carefully before you start.
2. Assemble all the ingredients on the counter.
3. Set out necessary cooking equipment, such as saucepans, skillets and wooden spoons. Preheat the oven and prepare cooking utensils – for example, butter a casserole dish or line a baking sheet with foil. This eliminates hunting through a drawer in the middle of a recipe to find a piece of equipment or waiting for the oven to preheat once the dish is ready to go.
4. Chop onions, garlic and vegetables before you start cooking. Place on a plate, tray or sheet of waxed paper within easy reach. Measure herbs, spices and seasonings; place in small custard cups or on plates.
5. Clean up as you go. Not only does this save time, you'll find it's far more efficient to work in an uncluttered kitchen.

You've got the basics covered, so turn the page and let's start cooking. Fast and easy does it!

Johanna Burkhard

NUTRITIONAL ANALYSIS NOTES

Computer-assisted nutrient analysis of the recipes in this book was performed by GOURMANIA INC., using the nutritional analysis software program The Food Processor® (version 7.11, April 1998) from ESHA Research, Salem, Oregon. The nutrient information was compiled from the latest USDA data, the 1997 Canadian Nutrient File, the Canadian Pork Council, and over 1,000 additional scientific notes.

The analysis was based on: Imperial measures and weights • the larger number of servings when there was a range • the smaller ingredient quantity when there was a range • the first ingredient listed when there was a choice.

Optional ingredients and ingredients in unspecified amounts were not included in the analysis. Nutrient values have been rounded to the nearest whole number (with exception of saturated fat, which has been rounded to one decimal place).

EASY NIBBLERS, SANDWICHES & SNACKS

SERVES 8

Always Popular Layered Bean Dip

Variations of the popular bean dip have been making the party circuit in recent years. Here's my updated version. It has an oregano/bean base, a creamy jalapeno cheese layer and a vibrant fresh topping of tomatoes, olives and coriander.

TIP

To make pita crisps, separate 3 (7-inch [18 cm]) thin pitas into rounds. Cut into 8 wedges each. Place in single layer on 2 baking sheets; bake in 350° F (180° C) oven for 8 to 10 minutes or until crisp and lightly toasted. Transfer to a rack to cool. Can be prepared up to a week ahead and stored in an airtight container or frozen.

8-INCH (20 CM) SHALLOW ROUND SERVING DISH OR PIE PLATE

1	can (19 oz [540 mL]) red kidney beans *or* black beans, rinsed and drained	1
1	clove garlic, minced	1
1 tsp	dried oregano	5 mL
1/2 tsp	ground cumin	2 mL
1 cup	shredded Monterey Jack or Cheddar cheese	250 mL
3/4 cup	light sour cream	175 mL
1 tbsp	minced pickled jalapeno peppers	15 mL
2	tomatoes, seeded and finely diced	2
1	Haas avocado, peeled and diced (optional)	1
2	green onions, finely chopped	2
1/3 cup	sliced black olives	75 mL
1/3 cup	chopped fresh coriander or parsley	75 mL

1. In a food processor, combine beans, garlic, oregano, cumin and 1 tbsp (15 mL) water; process until smooth. Spread in serving dish.
2. In a bowl combine cheese, sour cream and jalapeno peppers. Spread over bean layer. (Can be assembled earlier in day; cover and refrigerate.)
3. Just before serving, sprinkle with tomatoes, avocado (if using), green onions, olives and coriander. Serve with pita crisps (see note, at left).

Per serving (without avocado)	
Calories	175
Protein	10 g
Carbohydrates	18 g
Dietary Fiber	7 g
Fat - Total	7 g
Saturated Fat	4.3 g
Calcium	148 mg

**MAKES 1 1/2 CUPS
(375 ML)**

With a can of crab meat in the pantry and cream cheese in the fridge, you're all set to make a quick dip in 5 minutes flat. You can make it in the microwave or just as easily on the stovetop over medium heat.

TIP

Serve with Melba toast rounds or crisp vegetable dippers.

VARIATION

5-Minute Clam Dip
Substitute 1 can (5 oz [142 g]) drained clams for the crab. Stir in 1 minced garlic clove, if desired.

5-Minute Crab Dip

8 oz	light cream cheese	250 g
1	can (6 oz [170 mL]) crab meat, drained, liquid reserved	1
1/4 cup	finely chopped green onions	50 mL
2 tsp	freshly squeezed lemon juice	10 mL
1/2 tsp	Worcestershire sauce	2 mL
1/4 tsp	paprika	1 mL
	Hot pepper sauce	

1. Place cream cheese in a medium-sized microwave-safe bowl; microwave at Medium for 2 minutes or until softened. Stir until smooth.
2. Stir in crab, green onions, 2 tbsp (25 mL) reserved crab liquid, lemon juice, Worcestershire sauce, paprika and hot pepper sauce to taste. Microwave at Medium-High for 2 minutes or until piping hot. Serve warm.

Per tbsp (15 mL)	
Calories	24
Protein	2 g
Carbohydrates	1 g
Dietary Fiber	0 g
Fat - Total	1.4 g
Saturated Fat	1 g
Calcium	17 mg

When you've got the gang coming over, serve this warm dip and watch it disappear. I like to accompany it with white or blue corn tortilla chips.

TIP

Use 2 fresh jalapeno peppers instead of pickled. Or for a mild version, use 1 can (4 oz [113 g]) green chilies, drained and chopped.

To defrost spinach, remove packaging and place in 4-cup (1 L) casserole dish. Cover and microwave at High, stirring once, for 6 to 8 minutes or until defrosted and hot. Place in a sieve and press out excess moisture.

Warm Spinach and Cheese Dip

1	pkg (10 oz [300 g]) frozen chopped spinach, defrosted and squeezed dry	1
8 oz	light cream cheese, cubed and softened	250 g
1 cup	mild or medium salsa	250 mL
2	green onions, finely chopped	2
1	clove garlic, minced	1
1/2 tsp	dried oregano	2 mL
1/2 tsp	ground cumin	2 mL
1/2 cup	shredded Monterey Jack or Cheddar cheese	125 mL
1/2 cup	milk (approximate)	125 mL
	Salt	
	Hot pepper sauce	

1. In a medium saucepan, combine spinach, cream cheese, salsa, green onions, garlic, oregano and cumin. Cook over medium heat, stirring, for 2 to 3 minutes or until smooth and piping hot.
2. Stir in cheese and milk; cook for 2 minutes or until cheese melts. Add more milk to thin dip, if desired. Season with salt and hot pepper sauce to taste. Spoon into serving dish; accompany with tortilla chips.

MICROWAVE METHOD

In an 8-cup (2 L) casserole dish, combine spinach, cream cheese, salsa, onions, oregano and cumin; cover and microwave at Medium for 4 minutes, stirring once. Add cheese and milk; cover and microwave at Medium-High, stirring once, for 2 to 3 minutes, or until cheese is melted. Season with salt and hot pepper sauce to taste.

Per tbsp (15 mL)	
Calories	19
Protein	1 g
Carbohydrates	1 g
Dietary Fiber	0 g
Fat - Total	1 g
Saturated Fat	0.8 g
Calcium	28 mg

MAKES 2 CUPS (500 ML)

Do-Ahead Herb Dip

This creamy dip relies on low-fat dairy products and zesty herbs, so it clocks in with a lot less fat and calories than you might imagine. Make it at least a day ahead to let flavors develop. Serve with fresh veggies.

TIP

Other fresh herbs, including basil can be added according to what you have in the fridge or growing in your garden. If you're fond of fresh dill, increase the amount to 2 tbsp (25 mL).

This dip also makes a great dressing for pasta and potato salads. Store in a covered container in the fridge for up to 1 week.

1 cup	low-fat creamed cottage cheese	250 mL
1/2 cup	plain low-fat yogurt *or* light sour cream	125 mL
1/2 cup	light mayonnaise	125 mL
1/3 cup	finely chopped parsley	75 mL
2 tbsp	finely chopped chives *or* minced green onions	25 mL
1 tbsp	chopped fresh dill (or 1 tsp [15 mL] dried)	15 mL
1 1/2 tsp	Dijon mustard	7 mL
1 tsp	red wine vinegar *or* lemon juice	5 mL
	Hot pepper sauce	

1. In a food processor, purée cottage cheese, yogurt and mayonnaise until very smooth and creamy.
2. Transfer to a bowl; stir in parsley, chives, dill, mustard, vinegar and hot pepper sauce to taste. Cover and refrigerate.

Per tbsp (15 mL)	
Calories	20
Protein	1 g
Carbohydrates	1 g
Dietary Fiber	0 g
Fat - Total	1 g
Saturated Fat	0.4 g
Calcium	12 mg

Jalapeno Cheddar Toasts

Is it party time? Get a head start on your preparations with these tasty appetizers designed to be stored in the freezer. When the festivities are about to begin, just pop them into a hot oven.

PREHEAT OVEN TO 375° F (190° C)
BAKING SHEETS

8 oz	aged Cheddar cheese, shredded	250 g
1/2 cup	light cream cheese, cubed	125 mL
2 tbsp	finely diced red bell pepper	25 mL
2 tbsp	minced jalapeno peppers	25 mL
2 tbsp	finely chopped parsley	25 mL
36	baguette slices, cut 1/3-inch (8 mm) thick	36

TIP

To freeze, spread bread slices with cheese mixture; arrange in a single layer on baking sheets and freeze. Transfer to a rigid container, separating layers with waxed paper; freeze for up to 1 month. No need to defrost before baking.

Wear rubber gloves when handling jalapeno peppers to avoid skin irritation.

Use 1 tbsp (15 mL) minced pickled jalapeno peppers instead of fresh jalapeno peppers, if desired.

1. In a food processor, purée Cheddar and cream cheese until very smooth. Transfer to a bowl; stir in red pepper, jalapeno peppers and parsley.

2. Spread bread slices with a generous teaspoonful (5 mL) of cheese mixture; arrange on baking sheets.

3. Bake in oven for 10 to 12 minutes (up to 15 minutes if frozen) until tops are puffed and edges toasted. Serve warm.

Per toast	
Calories	51
Protein	2 g
Carbohydrates	5 g
Dietary Fiber	0 g
Fat - Total	2 g
Saturated Fat	1.3 g
Calcium	42 mg

Easy Artichoke Cheese Melts

Everyone likes to have a breezy appetizer in their repertoire. This is one of mine. It takes no time to prepare and tastes great.

TIP

Make this spread up to 3 days ahead, cover and refrigerate. Assemble appetizers just before serving or toasts will soften.

To lightly toast baguette slices, place on baking sheet in 375° F (190° C) oven for about 5 minutes.

PREHEAT OVEN TO 375° F (190° C)
BAKING SHEET

1	jar (6 oz [170 mL]) marinated artichokes, well-drained and finely chopped	1
1/2 cup	shredded Monterey Jack, Gouda or Cheddar cheese	125 mL
1/4 cup	grated Parmesan cheese	50 mL
1/4 cup	light mayonnaise	50 mL
24	baguette slices, cut 1/3 inch (8 mm) thick, lightly toasted	24
1/4 cup	finely diced red bell pepper	50 mL
8	Kalamata olives, cut into thin slivers	8

1. In a bowl combine artichokes, Monterey Jack, Parmesan and mayonnaise. Spread over toasts; top with red pepper and olive slivers.

2. Arrange on a baking sheet; bake for 10 to 12 minutes or until tops are bubbly and edges are golden. Serve warm.

Per cheese melt	
Calories	90
Protein	2 g
Carbohydrates	11 g
Dietary Fiber	1 g
Fat - Total	4 g
Saturated Fat	1.2 g
Calcium	35 mg

MAKES 36 APPETIZERS

Breezy Californian Quesadillas

Quesadillas sound complicated, but they are really just grilled sandwiches made with flour tortillas. The sky's the limit when it comes to fillings. This version, using roasted vegetables and goat cheese, is easy and delicious.

TIP

By the way, don't be intimidated by the fennel. It's simple to handle; just trim the top and cut in half lengthwise. Remove and discard the tough core.

Wraps can be assembled ahead. Cover in plastic wrap and refrigerate. Just pop them on the grill or in a nonstick skillet until toasted and cheese melts. Keep an eye on them – they cook quickly.

PREHEAT OVEN TO 400° F (200° C)
RIMMED BAKING SHEET, OILED

1	small red onion, diced	1
1	large red bell pepper, diced	1
Half	bulb fennel, cored and diced	Half
1 tbsp	olive oil (plus extra for grilling)	15 mL
1/2 tsp	salt	2 mL
1/2 tsp	pepper	2 mL
1/4 cup	chopped Kalamata olives	50 mL
1 tbsp	balsamic vinegar	15 mL
2 tbsp	chopped fresh basil	25 mL
6	flour tortillas (8-inch [20 cm] size)	6
6 oz	creamy goat cheese *or* light cream cheese, softened	175 g

1. Spread onion, red pepper and fennel on baking sheet. Drizzle with oil; season with salt and pepper. Roast in oven for 20 minutes, stirring occasionally, until vegetables are tender-crisp. Transfer to a bowl. Stir in olives and vinegar. Cover and refrigerate. (Can be made up to 3 days ahead.) Stir in basil.

2. Spread each tortilla with 2 tbsp (25 mL) of the goat cheese. Sprinkle each half with 1/4 cup (50 mL) of the vegetable mixture; fold over filling, pressing down lightly. (Can be assembled ahead, wrapped in plastic wrap and refrigerated for up to 4 hours.)

3. Brush quesadillas lightly with oil. Place on greased grill over medium heat or cook in batches in a large nonstick skillet over medium heat for 2 minutes on each side or until toasted. Cut each into 6 wedges. Serve warm.

Per wedge	
Calories	46
Protein	2 g
Carbohydrates	5 g
Dietary Fiber	0 g
Fat - Total	2 g
Saturated Fat	0.8 g
Calcium	13 mg

MAKES 2 1/2 CUPS (625 ML)

Ratatouille Salsa

Supermarket shelves are lined with great-tasting salsas. Take your favorite salsa, throw in a few roasted vegetables and voila! — you've got yourself a snazzy spread.

TIP

Prepare ratatouille salsa ahead. It keeps well in a covered container in the refrigerator for 3 days, or 1 month in the freezer.

This versatile sauce makes a wonderful condiment for sandwiches with cold cuts or cheese, or as a pizza topping. It's also a great filling for BREEZY CALIFORNIAN QUESADILLAS (see recipe, page 24).

Dice the vegetables into uniform 1/4-inch (5 mm) pieces.

Medium salsa gives a nice burst of heat to the sauce. If using mild salsa, add hot pepper sauce such as Tabasco to taste.

PREHEAT OVEN TO 425° F (220° C)
RIMMED BAKING SHEET, OILED

1 1/2 cups	diced eggplant	375 mL
1 1/2 cups	diced zucchini	375 mL
1	red bell pepper, diced	1
1 tsp	dried basil	5 mL
1 tbsp	olive oil	15 mL
1 1/2 cups	medium salsa	375 mL
1/4 cup	chopped parsley	50 mL
1	clove garlic, minced	1

1. Spread eggplant, zucchini and red pepper on baking sheet. Sprinkle with basil; drizzle with oil. Roast in oven, stirring occasionally, for about 20 minutes or until vegetables are tender and lightly colored.
2. Transfer to a bowl; stir in salsa, parsley and garlic. Cover and refrigerate.

Per tbsp (15 mL)	
Calories	6
Protein	0 g
Carbohydrates	1 g
Dietary Fiber	0 g
Fat - Total	0 g
Saturated Fat	0 g
Calcium	5 mg

Here's a more appealing version of nachos and cheese — and it's lower in fat.

Per nacho	
Calories	21
Protein	1 g
Carbohydrates	1 g
Dietary Fiber	0 g
Fat - Total	2 g
Saturated Fat	0.8 g
Calcium	47 mg

These hearty appetizers pack a mighty taste. Serve on grilled bread or toasted baguette slices.

Toasted baguette slices

Cut 1 thin baguette (French bread) into 1/3-inch (8 mm) thick slices. Arrange on baking sheet; brush lightly with 2 tbsp (25 mL) olive oil or a herb-infused oil. Bake in 375° F (190° C) oven for 5 minutes or until edges are lightly toasted.

Per serving	
Calories	144
Protein	4 g
Carbohydrates	18 g
Dietary Fiber	2 g
Fat - Total	6 g
Saturated Fat	1.9 g
Calcium	71 mg

Ratatouille Nachos

PREHEAT BROILER
BAKING SHEET

24	round nacho tortilla chips	24
1 cup	RATATOUILLE SALSA (see recipe, page 25)	250 mL
1 cup	shredded mild Asiago or Provolone cheese	250 mL

1. Arrange nachos in a single layer on baking sheet. Top each with about 2 tsp (10 mL) salsa; sprinkle with cheese. Place under preheated broiler for 2 minutes or until cheese melts. Watch carefully; serve warm.

Ratatouille Bruschetta with Feta

PREHEAT BARBECUE GRILL OR BROILER

6	thick slices crusty Italian bread	6
1 tbsp	olive oil	15 mL
1 cup	RATATOUILLE SALSA (see recipe, page 25)	250 mL
1/3 cup	finely crumbled feta cheese	75 mL
6	Kalamata olives, pitted and slivered	6

1. Toast both sides of bread on a barbecue grill or under broiler; brush one side lightly with olive oil. Spread with salsa; sprinkle with feta cheese and Kalamata olive slivers. Cut into halves, if desired. Serve immediately.

SERVES 4

Greek Chicken Pita Sandwiches

When I'm in the mood for something easy for dinner, this is what I make. It beats sandwiches or burgers from fast food restaurants hands down.

TIP

A combination of lemon juice, garlic and oregano is the classic marinade for souvlaki. I also use it as a quick marinade combined with 1 tbsp (15 mL) olive oil to brush-over chicken breasts and pork loin chops on the barbecue.

1 lb	skinless, boneless chicken breasts, cut into very thin strips	500 g
1 tbsp	freshly squeezed lemon juice	15 mL
1	large clove garlic, minced	1
3/4 tsp	dried oregano	4 mL
1/4 tsp	salt	1 mL
1/4 tsp	pepper	1 mL
2 tsp	olive oil	10 mL
1	small red onion, halved lengthwise and thinly sliced	1
1	red or green bell pepper, cut into 2-inch (5 cm) thin strips	1
4	pitas (7-inch [18 cm] size), halved to make pockets	4
3/4 cup	TZATZIKI SAUCE (store-bought or see recipe, page 146)	175 mL
4 cups	shredded romaine lettuce	1 L
2	tomatoes, cut into wedges	2

1. In a bowl combine chicken, lemon juice, garlic, oregano, salt and pepper; marinate at room temperature for 10 minutes.

2. In a large nonstick skillet, heat oil over high heat; cook chicken, stirring, for 2 to 3 minutes or until no longer pink. Add onion and bell pepper; cook, stirring, for 2 minutes or until vegetables are softened.

3. Wrap pitas in paper towels; microwave at Medium for 1 1/2 minutes or until warm. Spoon chicken mixture into pita halves; top with a generous spoonful of TZATZIKI SAUCE, shredded lettuce and tomato wedges.

Per serving	
Calories	375
Protein	33 g
Carbohydrates	46 g
Dietary Fiber	4 g
Fat - Total	6 g
Saturated Fat	1.3 g
Calcium	160 mg

Spicy Thai Shrimp

Tired of traditional shrimp and red cocktail sauce? Try this spicy way to serve shrimp instead. Wrap the shrimp in snow peas, if you wish, or set out the bowl of marinated shrimp and let guests help themselves.

TIP

If using raw shrimp, plunge into a large saucepan of boiling salted water. Cook just until water returns to a full rolling boil and shrimp turn pink. Drain; rinse shrimp under cold water to chill. Peel and devein, but leave tail intact.

2 tbsp	freshly squeezed lime juice	25 mL
2 tbsp	Thai fish sauce *or* soya sauce	25 mL
2 tsp	brown sugar	10 mL
1	large clove garlic, minced	1
1/2 tsp	red pepper flakes	2 mL
2 tbsp	chopped fresh coriander *or* parsley	25 mL
1 lb	large cooked shrimp, peeled, deveined, tails left on (about 30)	500 g
30	snow peas, ends trimmed	30

1. In a bowl combine lime juice, fish sauce, brown sugar, garlic, red pepper flakes and coriander. Add shrimp and toss well. Cover and refrigerate, stirring occasionally, for 1 hour or up to 1 day ahead.

2. In a medium saucepan, blanch snow peas in boiling salted water for 1 minute or until bright green and pliable; do not overcook. Drain; rinse under cold water to chill. (Can be done earlier in day.) Wrap a snow pea around each shrimp; secure with a toothpick. Arrange on serving platter; garnish with additional coriander.

Per appetizer	
Calories	19
Protein	4 g
Carbohydrates	1 g
Dietary Fiber	0 g
Fat - Total	0 g
Saturated Fat	0 g
Calcium	8 mg

**MAKES 24
APPETIZERS**

Everyone loves smoked salmon and these popular appetizers are always the first to go at a party.

TIP

Can be made earlier in the day or even the day ahead – just cover and refrigerate. Garnish shortly before serving.

Use this cream cheese and mustard spread instead of mayonnaise when you're making finger sandwiches with sliced smoked ham or turkey.

Irresistible Smoked Salmon Bites

1/2 cup	light cream cheese	125 mL
1 tbsp	finely chopped fresh dill	15 mL
2 tsp	honey mustard	10 mL
2 tsp	grainy mustard	10 mL
2 tsp	freshly squeezed lemon juice	10 mL
6	slices dark rye or pumpernickel bread, crusts trimmed	6
6 oz	sliced smoked salmon	175 g
	Capers and dill sprigs for garnish	

1. Place cream cheese in a bowl; microwave at Medium for 1 minute to soften. Stir well. Blend in dill, honey mustard, grainy mustard and lemon juice.

2. Generously spread mustard mixture over bread slices; layer with smoked salmon. Cut each slice into 4 triangles or squares, or 6 rectangles. Garnish with capers and dill. Cover with plastic wrap and refrigerate.

Per appetizer	
Calories	43
Protein	3 g
Carbohydrates	5 g
Dietary Fiber	1 g
Fat - Total	2 g
Saturated Fat	0.7 g
Calcium	14 mg

MAKES 20 APPETIZERS

Here are tasty nibblers that do double duty as appetizers or as bite-size sandwiches for afternoon tea.

TIP

Simmer 2 boneless chicken breasts in lightly salted water or chicken stock for 10 minutes; remove from heat. Let cool in poaching broth for 15 minutes. Assemble sandwiches shortly before serving to prevent lettuce from wilting.

Mini Pitas with Curried Chicken

1/3 cup	light mayonnaise	75 mL
2 tbsp	mango chutney	25 mL
1 tsp	curry powder	5 mL
1 1/2 cups	finely diced cooked chicken	375 mL
1/2 cup	finely diced unpeeled apple	125 mL
1/3 cup	finely diced radishes	75 mL
2 tbsp	finely chopped green onions	25 mL
	Salt	
10	mini pitas (3-inch [8 cm] size)	10
	Red leaf or Boston lettuce	

1. In a bowl, blend mayonnaise, chutney and curry powder until smooth. Stir in chicken, apple, radishes and green onions; season with salt to taste.
2. Cut pitas in half to make pockets. Line each pocket with lettuce; spoon in chicken mixture. Arrange on serving plate.

Per appetizer	
Calories	71
Protein	5 g
Carbohydrates	9 g
Dietary Fiber	1 g
Fat - Total	2 g
Saturated Fat	0.4 g
Calcium	14 mg

Wraps have taken the country by storm as a healthy fast food craze. Anything goes when making these California-inspired tortilla-wrapped sandwiches including rice or grains, or grilled meats and vegetables with tangy spreads and salsas. Here is a kid-friendly wrap that's fun to eat and makes a great supper.

TIP

If you have cooked white or brown rice handy in the fridge, you'll need 2 cups (500 mL) for this recipe.

Omit sausages for a vegetarian version. The larger-size flour tortillas (10-inch [25 cm]) also work well in this recipe.

These wraps are great to assemble ahead and reheat in the microwave. Wrap sandwiches individually in paper towels. Microwave 3 at a time at Medium for 4 minutes, or microwave 1 wrap at Medium for 1 1/2 minutes or until heated through.

Per wrap	
Calories	472
Protein	21 g
Carbohydrates	54 g
Dietary Fiber	3 g
Fat - Total	19 g
Saturated Fat	6.6 g
Calcium	237 mg

All-New Sausage Rice Wraps

PREHEAT OVEN TO 350° F (180° C)
BAKING SHEETS

1 1/2 cups	chicken stock or vegetable stock	375 mL
2/3 cup	long-grain white rice	150 mL
12 oz	mild or hot Italian sausages, casings removed	375 g
2 tsp	olive oil	10 mL
1	small onion, chopped	1
2	cloves garlic, minced	2
1	large green bell pepper, chopped	1
1 cup	chopped mushrooms	250 mL
1 1/2 tsp	dried oregano or basil	7 mL
1 cup	bottled tomato pasta sauce	250 mL
6	flour tortillas (8 inch [20 cm] size)	6
1 1/2 cups	shredded part-skim mozzarella or Fontina cheese	375 mL

1. In a saucepan, bring stock to a boil; stir in rice. Reduce heat to low, cover and simmer for 20 minutes or until tender. Uncover; fluff with a fork.

2. In a large nonstick skillet, cook sausage meat over medium-high heat, breaking up with a wooden spoon, for 5 minutes or until no longer pink. Drain in sieve to remove excess fat; set aside.

3. Add oil to skillet; reduce heat to medium. Add onion, garlic, green pepper, mushrooms and oregano; cook, stirring, for 4 minutes or until softened. Add hot cooked rice, sausage and tomato pasta sauce; cook for 2 minutes or until heated through.

4. Place tortillas on baking sheets; sprinkle with cheese. Bake for 4 minutes or until cheese is melted. Spread about 3/4 cup (175 mL) filling in a 2- by 5-inch (5 by 12 cm) rectangle along bottom half of each tortilla. Fold 1 inch (2.5 cm) of the left and right sides over filling. Starting from bottom, roll up tortillas around filling. Serve warm.

SERVES 4

I've taken the classic BLT and fashioned it into a wrap, adding fresh basil to the mayonnaise for a thoroughly modern twist.

TIP

If tomatoes aren't fully ripened when you buy them, place in a paper bag on your counter for a day a two. The ethylene gas given off by the tomatoes speeds up the ripening process.

Never store tomatoes in the fridge – the cold temperature numbs their sweet flavor.

A sunny window sill may seem like a good place to ripen tomatoes, but a hot sun often bakes rather than ripens them.

VARIATION

Club Wrap

Cut 2 grilled or cooked chicken breasts into thin strips. Spread tortillas with basil mayonnaise; layer with tomato, lettuce, chicken and bacon. Roll tortillas as directed.

Per wrap	
Calories	341
Protein	17 g
Carbohydrates	35 g
Dietary Fiber	4 g
Fat - Total	15 g
Saturated Fat	3.3 g
Calcium	55 mg

It's a BLT Wrap!

8	slices bacon, cut into quarters	8
1/3 cup	light mayonnaise	75 mL
2 tbsp	chopped fresh basil (or 1/2 tsp [2 mL] dried)	25 mL
4	flour tortillas (8-inch [20 cm] size)	4
2	large tomatoes	2
4 cups	shredded romaine lettuce	1 L

1. Place bacon on a microwave-safe rack or on a large plate lined with a double layer of paper towels; loosely cover with another layer of paper towels. Microwave at High for 5 minutes or until cooked and almost crisp. Let cool.

2. In a bowl combine mayonnaise and basil. Spread over tortillas leaving a 1-inch (2.5 cm) border around edge. Cut tomatoes in half crosswise and gently squeeze out seeds; slice thinly. Layer tortillas with tomato slices, lettuce and bacon. Fold 1-inch (2.5 cm) of the right and left sides of tortilla over filling; starting from the bottom, roll tortillas around filling. Serve immediately or cover in plastic wrap and store in the refrigerator for up to 1 day.

GREEK CHICKEN PITA SANDWICHES (PAGE 27) »

MAKES 8

Mexican dishes are a big hit with teens — and their parents. I designed this recipe for my vegetarian daughter. It makes a nourishing snack or supper. For a meat version, add strips of ham, cooked turkey or chicken.

TIP

Make a batch of burritos, wrap each in a paper towel, then in plastic wrap. Keep handy in the fridge for microwaveable school lunches or after-school snacks. Remove plastic wrap before microwaving.

Black Bean Vegetable Burritos

1 tbsp	vegetable oil	15 mL
3	green onions, chopped	3
1	large clove garlic, minced	1
1 cup	diced zucchini	250 mL
1	red or green bell pepper, chopped	1
1 tsp	dried oregano	5 mL
1 tsp	ground cumin	5 mL
1	can (19 oz [540 mL]) black beans *or* kidney beans, rinsed and well-drained	1
8	flour tortillas, (8-inch [20 cm] size), preferably whole wheat	8
1 cup	shredded part-skim mozzarella or Cheddar cheese	250 mL
1 cup	mild or medium salsa	250 mL
1/2 cup	light sour cream	125 mL

1. In a large nonstick skillet, heat oil over medium heat. Add green onions, garlic, zucchini, bell pepper, oregano and cumin; cook, stirring, for 5 minutes or until vegetables are tender-crisp. Stir in beans; cook 1 to 2 minutes or until heated through.

2. Spoon 1/4 cup (50 mL) of the bean mixture down the middle of each tortilla. Top each with 2 tbsp (25 mL) shredded cheese, 2 tbsp (25 mL) salsa and 1 tbsp (15 mL) sour cream. Roll to enclose filling. Wrap each burrito in a paper towel. Place 4 at a time on a plate; microwave at Medium-High for 3 to 4 minutes or until heated through. To heat a single burrito, microwave at Medium-High for 1 minute.

Per burrito	
Calories	300
Protein	13 g
Carbohydrates	42 g
Dietary Fiber	7 g
Fat - Total	9 g
Saturated Fat	3.1 g
Calcium	177 mg

◄ BIG BATCH VEGETABLE MINESTRONE(PAGE 38)

Why order out when it's so easy to prepare these pizza-style sandwiches at home? Make them with leftover grilled steak or store-bought deli roast beef for a fast dinner.

TIP

Prepare sandwich filling ahead, cover and refrigerate. Layer rolls with cheese; spoon in beef filling. Wrap in paper towels and microwave at Medium-High for 2 1/2 to 3 minutes for 2 rolls, or 1 1/2 minutes for 1 roll, or until heated through.

Beefy Pizza Subs

PREHEAT BROILER
BAKING SHEET

1 tbsp	olive oil	15 mL
2 cups	sliced mushrooms	500 mL
1	green bell pepper, cut into thin strips	1
1	medium onion, cut into thin wedges	1
1	large clove garlic, minced	1
1 tsp	dried basil *or* oregano	5 mL
1/4 tsp	red pepper flakes	1 mL
1 1/2 cups	thinly sliced cooked flank steak *or* 6 oz (175 g) deli roast beef, cut into strips	375 mL
3/4 cup	pizza sauce or tomato pasta sauce	175 mL
	Salt and pepper	
4	crusty rolls (8-inch [20 cm] length)	4
6 oz	thinly sliced mild provolone or mozzarella cheese	175 g

1. In a large nonstick skillet, heat oil over medium-high heat. Add mushrooms, green pepper, onion, garlic, basil and red pepper flakes; cook, stirring, for 5 minutes or until softened. Stir in beef and pizza sauce; cook until heated through. Remove from heat; season with salt and pepper to taste.

2. Cut rolls along 1 side and open; layer with cheese slices. Place on baking sheet under preheated broiler for 1 minute or until cheese melts. Watch carefully. Spoon beef mixture into rolls.

Per sub	
Calories	501
Protein	27 g
Carbohydrates	48 g
Dietary Fiber	4 g
Fat - Total	22 g
Saturated Fat	11.1 g
Calcium	414 mg

Soups & Chowders

SERVES 4

In-a-Hurry Tortellini Soup

Serve this soup with crusty French bread and you'll have a nourishing supper that takes only about 30 minutes to make.

TIP

Instead of frozen vegetables, add the same quantity of fresh vegetables — including chopped carrots, celery, zucchini and cauliflower — at the same time the pasta goes in the pot.

2 tsp	olive oil	10 mL
1	small onion, finely chopped	1
2	cloves garlic, minced	2
1 tsp	dried basil	5 mL
3 cups	chicken stock	750 mL
1	can (14 oz [398 mL]) tomatoes, chopped	1
2 cups	cheese- or meat-filled tortellini (fresh or frozen)	500 mL
2 cups	frozen mixed Italian vegetables	500 mL
	Salt and pepper	
	Grated Parmesan cheese	

1. In a large saucepan, heat oil over medium heat. Add onion, garlic and basil; cook, stirring, for 2 minutes or until softened. Add chicken stock and tomatoes; bring to a boil. Add tortellini. Reduce heat to medium; cover and cook, stirring occasionally, for 5 minutes.

2. Add frozen vegetables; cover and cook for another 8 minutes, or until pasta and vegetables are just tender. Season with salt and pepper to taste. Ladle into soup bowls; sprinkle generously with Parmesan cheese.

Per serving	
Calories	306
Protein	16 g
Carbohydrates	44 g
Dietary Fiber	6 g
Fat - Total	8 g
Saturated Fat	3 g
Calcium	209 mg

Quick Chickpea and Pasta Soup

Soup's on! Your fridge may be bare, but chances are you'll have the basic ingredients in your pantry to make this sustaining main-course soup for a quick-fix dinner.

TIP

Other types of canned beans or lentils can be used instead of chickpeas.

VARIATION

Chickpea, Pasta and Spinach Soup
Increase stock to 6 cups (1.5 L). Stir in 4 cups (1 L) shredded fresh spinach or Swiss chard, along with chickpeas and pasta.

1 tbsp	olive oil	15 mL
1	medium onion, chopped	1
2	cloves garlic, finely chopped	2
1/2 tsp	dried basil *or* Italian herbs	2 mL
2 tbsp	tomato paste	25 mL
5 cups	chicken stock *or* vegetable stock (approximate)	1.25 L
3/4 cup	small pasta shapes such as shells	175 mL
1	can (19 oz [540 mL]) chickpeas, rinsed and drained	1
	Salt and pepper	
	Grated Parmesan cheese	

1. In a large saucepan, heat oil over medium heat. Add onion, garlic and basil; cook, stirring, for 2 minutes or until softened. Add tomato paste; cook, stirring for 30 seconds.

2. Add stock; bring to a boil. Stir in pasta and chickpeas; partially cover and cook, stirring occasionally, for 8 to 10 minutes or until pasta is just tender. Season with salt and pepper to taste. Ladle soup into bowls and serve sprinkled with Parmesan cheese.

Per serving	
Calories	314
Protein	16 g
Carbohydrates	47 g
Dietary Fiber	7 g
Fat - Total	7 g
Saturated Fat	1.2 g
Calcium	73 mg

SERVES 8

I always make a double batch of this soup each fall when vegetables are at their prime. I pack it into containers and put in the freezer for easy mid-week meals on chilly days. Any combination of vegetables can be used in this hearty vegetable soup, depending on what's in your fridge. SUN-DRIED TOMATO PESTO is optional (see recipe, page 124), but it adds a wonderful jolt of flavor and dresses up the soup. You can also use whatever pesto you have on hand.

TIP

Serve with additional Parmesan cheese at the table.

Refrigerate soup for up to 5 days or freeze in airtight containers for up to 3 months.

Per serving (without pesto)	
Calories	223
Protein	15 g
Carbohydrates	32 g
Dietary Fiber	8 g
Fat - Total	4 g
Saturated Fat	0.9 g
Calcium	89 mg

Big Batch Vegetable Minestrone

1 tbsp	olive oil	15 mL
2	large onions, chopped	2
3	cloves garlic, finely chopped	3
2	carrots, peeled and chopped	2
2	stalks celery, chopped	2
10 cups	vegetable stock or chicken stock (approximate)	2.5 L
2 cups	shredded cabbage	500 mL
2 cups	small cauliflower florets	500 mL
1/3 cup	short fine noodles or other small pasta shapes such as shells	75 mL
1 cup	frozen peas	250 mL
1	can (19 oz [540 mL]) romano or navy beans, rinsed and drained	1
3/4 cup	SUN-DRIED TOMATO PESTO (see recipe, page 124) or 1/4 cup [50 mL] chopped parsley	175 mL
	Grated Parmesan cheese (optional)	

1. In a large stockpot or 32-cup (8 L) Dutch oven, heat oil over medium heat. Add onions, garlic, carrots and celery; cook, stirring occasionally, for 10 minutes or until softened.

2. Add stock and cabbage; bring to a boil over high heat. Reduce heat, cover and simmer for 20 minutes or just until vegetables are tender. Stir in cauliflower and pasta; simmer, covered, for 8 minutes or just until pasta is tender. Stir in peas and beans; cook for 2 minutes.

3. Ladle into bowls; swirl a generous tablespoon (15 mL) SUN-DRIED TOMATO PESTO into each, or garnish soup with chopped parsley. Sprinkle with Parmesan cheese, if desired. Soup thickens slightly as it cools; add more stock, if necessary.

Creamy Carrot Orange Soup

Looking for a great opener for a meal? Here it is. The sweetness of carrots and orange are balanced by the tang of yogurt in this low-calorie soup.

TIP

Normally yogurt will curdle if you add it to a soup or sauce, but blending it with cornstarch as a binder overcomes this problem.

1 tbsp	vegetable oil	15 mL
1	medium onion, chopped	1
1	large clove garlic, finely chopped	1
2 tsp	curry powder	10 mL
4 cups	sliced carrots	1 L
4 cups	chicken stock	1 L
1 cup	orange juice	250 mL
1 cup	plain low-fat yogurt	250 mL
1 tbsp	cornstarch	15 mL
	Salt and pepper	
2 tbsp	chopped parsley *or* chives	25 mL
	Grated orange zest	

1. In a large saucepan, heat oil over medium heat. Add onion, garlic and curry powder; cook, stirring, for 2 minutes or until softened. Add carrots, chicken stock and orange juice. Bring to a boil; cover and simmer for 45 minutes or until carrots are very tender. Let cool 10 minutes.

2. In a blender or food processor, purée in batches; return to saucepan. In a bowl, blend yogurt with cornstarch; stir into soup. Cook over medium heat, stirring, for 5 minutes or until heated through. Season with salt and pepper to taste. Ladle into bowls; sprinkle with parsley and orange zest.

Per serving	
Calories	153
Protein	7 g
Carbohydrates	22 g
Dietary Fiber	4 g
Fat - Total	4 g
Saturated Fat	0.9 g
Calcium	128 mg

SERVES 4 AS A MAIN COURSE OR 6 AS A STARTER

Corn and Red Pepper Chowder

Sweet, young corn, combined with tender leeks and bell pepper, make a delicately flavored fall soup. Kernels cut from cooked cobs of corn are ideal for this recipe. You'll need about 3 cobs.

TIP

To cut kernels from the cob easily, stand the ears on end and use a sharp knife.

1 tbsp	butter	15 mL
2	medium leeks, white and light green part only, finely chopped	2
1/2 tsp	dried thyme	2 mL
2 1/2 cups	chicken stock *or* vegetable stock	625 mL
1 1/2 cups	cooked or frozen corn kernels	375 mL
1	large red bell pepper, diced	1
3 tbsp	all-purpose flour	45 mL
2 cups	milk	500 mL
	Salt and pepper	
2 tbsp	chopped parsley *or* chives	25 mL

1. In a large saucepan, melt butter over medium heat. Add leeks and thyme; cook, stirring often, for 4 minutes or until softened. Do not brown. Stir in stock and, if using, frozen corn. Bring to a boil; reduce heat, cover and simmer for 10 minutes. Add cooked corn, if using, and red pepper; cover and simmer for 5 minutes or until vegetables are tender.

2. In a bowl, blend flour with 1/3 cup (75 mL) of the milk to make a smooth paste; stir in remaining milk. Stir into saucepan; bring to a boil, stirring, until thickened. Season with salt and pepper to taste. Ladle into soup bowls; sprinkle with parsley or chives.

Per serving (6)	
Calories	147
Protein	7 g
Carbohydrates	21 g
Dietary Fiber	2 g
Fat - Total	5 g
Saturated Fat	2.4 g
Calcium	123 mg

One-Dish Oriental Beef Noodle Soup

Loaded with vegetables, this soup is low in calories and full of flavor. A brimming bowlful makes a great meal-in-one supper that takes less than 10 minutes to cook.

TIP

Assemble and prepare all ingredients before you begin cooking.

To pull apart rice noodles, place bundle of noodles in a paper bag to prevent them from flying all over the kitchen. Angel hair pasta can be substituted for the rice noodles.

8 oz	lean tender beef (such as sirloin), cut into very thin strips	250 g
2 tbsp	soya sauce	25 mL
8 cups	beef stock	2 L
2	thin slices ginger root, smashed with side of knife	2
2 cups	rice vermicelli, broken into 3-inch (8 cm) pieces	500 mL
2	medium carrots, peeled and shredded	2
2 cups	sliced Chinese (napa) cabbage	500 mL
2 cups	mung bean sprouts	500 mL
1/4 cup	chopped fresh coriander	50 mL
2	green onions, chopped	2
	Toasted sesame oil (optional)	

1. In a bowl combine beef strips with soya sauce. Set aside.

2. In a large saucepan, combine stock and ginger; bring to a boil over high heat. Add vermicelli and boil for 2 to 3 minutes or until just tender. Add beef-soya mixture, carrots and cabbage.

3. Return to a boil; cook for 2 minutes. Add bean sprouts; cook 1 minute or until heated through. Ladle into soup bowls; garnish with coriander and green onions. Season with toasted sesame oil, if desired.

Per serving (6)	
Calories	275
Protein	16 g
Carbohydrates	44 g
Dietary Fiber	2 g
Fat - Total	3 g
Saturated Fat	1.4 g
Calcium	53 mg

Super Suppertime Lentil Soup

Of all dried legumes, lentils are my favorite. They're fast and easy to cook – and healthy too! With this soup, I bring the stock to a boil, throw in some vegetables, sit back, relax and savor the aroma. In 40 minutes, I am ladling out bowlfuls of wholesome soup.

TIP

To save time, I chop the mushrooms, onions, carrots and celery in batches in the food processor. If you have any leftover baked ham, chop it and add to the soup along with the stock.

8 cups	chicken stock *or* vegetable stock	2 L
1 cup	green lentils, rinsed and sorted	250 mL
8 oz	mushrooms, chopped	250 g
2	carrots, peeled and chopped	2
2	stalks celery with leaves, chopped	2
1	large onion, chopped	1
2	cloves garlic, finely chopped	2
1 tsp	dried thyme or marjoram	5 mL
1/4 cup	chopped fresh dill *or* parsley	50 mL
	Salt and pepper	

1. In a large Dutch oven or stockpot, combine stock, lentils, mushrooms, carrots, celery, onion, garlic and thyme.
2. Bring to a boil; reduce heat, cover and simmer 35 to 40 minutes or until lentils are tender. Stir in dill or parsley. Adjust seasoning with salt and pepper to taste.

Per serving	
Calories	180
Protein	15 g
Carbohydrates	25 g
Dietary Fiber	10 g
Fat - Total	2 g
Saturated Fat	0.6 g
Calcium	55 mg

Hearty Creole Fish Soup

The trademark seasonings of Creole cooking — onions, green pepper and celery — have been combined in a tomato and cream base to create this luscious fish soup.

TIP

Any kind of fish – such as cod, sole, haddock or bluefish – can be used.

If using frozen fish, remove packaging and arrange fish on plate; microwave at High for 3 to 4 minutes or until partially defrosted. Cut fish into small cubes; let stand 15 minutes to complete defrosting.

1 tbsp	olive oil	15 mL
4	green onions, chopped	4
1	large clove garlic, minced	1
2	stalks celery with leaves, chopped	2
1	green bell pepper, diced	1
1 tsp	paprika	5 mL
1/2 tsp	dried thyme	2 mL
Pinch	cayenne pepper	Pinch
2 cups	diced peeled potatoes	500 mL
1	can (19 oz [540 mL]) stewed tomatoes, chopped	1
2 cups	fish stock *or* vegetable stock (approximate)	500 mL
1 lb	fresh or frozen fish fillets	500 g
1/2 cup	whipping (35%) cream (optional)	125 mL
	Salt and pepper	

1. In a large saucepan, heat oil over medium heat. Add green onions, garlic, celery, green pepper, paprika, thyme and cayenne; cook, stirring, for 3 minutes or until softened. Add potatoes, stewed tomatoes and stock; bring to a boil. Reduce heat, cover and simmer for 15 minutes or until vegetables are tender.

2. Add fish; simmer for 2 minutes or until fish flakes when tested with a fork. Stir in cream, if using. (Add more stock if soup is too thick.) Season with salt and pepper to taste.

Per serving (6) (without cream)

Calories	178
Protein	17 g
Carbohydrates	20 g
Dietary Fiber	3 g
Fat - Total	4 g
Saturated Fat	0.7 g
Calcium	66 mg

SERVES 4

A bowlful of this chowder provides a boost of calcium for people who may not be big milk drinkers. Remove any skin in canned salmon but mash the calcium-rich bones and add to soup.

TIP

I prefer to use canned sockeye salmon as it gives a richer color to the chowder. You can also use I cup (250 mL) poached fresh salmon instead of canned.

Dill Salmon Chowder

1		can (7 1/2 oz [213 g]) salmon	1
1 tbsp		butter	15 mL
1		small onion, finely chopped	1
1 1/2 cups		diced peeled potatoes	375 mL
1 cup		diced peeled carrots	250 mL
1 cup		chicken stock *or* fish stock	250 mL
2 tbsp		all-purpose flour	25 mL
2 cups		milk	500 mL
2 tbsp		chopped fresh dill *or* parsley (or 1 tsp [5 mL] dried)	25 mL
		Salt and pepper	

1. Drain salmon, reserving liquid. Discard any skin; flake salmon and mash bones with fork. Set aside.

2. In a medium saucepan, melt butter over medium heat. Add onion, potatoes and carrots; cook, stirring often, for 5 minutes or until softened. Add stock and reserved salmon liquid; bring to a boil. Reduce heat, cover and simmer for 15 minutes or until vegetables are tender.

3. In a bowl, blend flour with 1/3 cup (75 mL) of the milk to make a smooth paste; stir in remaining milk. Stir into soup; bring to a boil, stirring often, until slightly thickened. Stir in salmon and dill; cook for 1 to 2 minutes or until piping hot. Season with salt and pepper to taste.

Per serving	
Calories	266
Protein	18 g
Carbohydrates	26 g
Dietary Fiber	3 g
Fat - Total	10 g
Saturated Fat	4.3 g
Calcium	300 mg

SERVES 4 TO 5

Lemon Broccoli Soup

Equally good served hot or cold, this soup has a pleasing spiciness imparted by cumin. I normally rely on milk for its creamy texture, but I like to splurge and add cream when I serve this soup for a special meal.

TIP

This is a more delicate soup which relies on potatoes and broccoli rather than flour as a thickener. Be sure not to let it boil once the milk has been added or the soup may curdle.

1 tbsp	butter	15 mL
1	large onion, chopped	1
1	large clove garlic, finely chopped	1
1 tsp	ground cumin *or* coriander *or* curry powder	5 mL
5 cups	broccoli florets with peeled and chopped stalks	1.25 L
1 1/2 cups	diced peeled potatoes	375 mL
3 cups	chicken stock *or* vegetable stock	750 mL
1 cup	milk or light (10%) cream	250 mL
1 tsp	grated lemon zest	5 mL
	Salt and pepper	
2 tbsp	chopped fresh chives or green onions	25 mL

1. In a large saucepan, melt butter over medium heat. Add onion, garlic and cumin; cook, stirring, for 2 minutes or until softened. Add broccoli, potatoes and stock; bring to a boil. Reduce heat, cover and simmer for 25 minutes or until vegetables are very tender. Let cool slightly.

2. In a food processor or blender, purée soup in batches until smooth. Return to saucepan; add milk and lemon zest. Season with salt and pepper to taste. Heat until piping hot; do not let boil. Ladle into bowls; sprinkle with chives.

Per serving (5)	
Calories	149
Protein	9 g
Carbohydrates	20 g
Dietary Fiber	4 g
Fat - Total	5 g
Saturated Fat	2.3 g
Calcium	122 mg

SERVES 6

Harvest Vegetable Barley Soup

Here's a main course soup to serve with whole grain bread and a wedge of Cheddar. Vary the soup according to the kinds of vegetables you have in the fridge. I often add small cauliflower and broccoli florets or a handful of chopped fresh spinach.

TIP

Instead of sweet potatoes, add 1 cup (250 mL) each diced peeled potatoes and diced carrots. Add along with the rutabaga.

2 tbsp	butter	25 mL
1	large onion, chopped	1
3	cloves garlic, finely chopped	3
1 1/2 cups	diced peeled rutabaga	375 mL
1/2 tsp	dried thyme or marjoram	2 mL
8 cups	chicken stock *or* vegetable stock (approximate)	2 L
1/2 cup	pearl barley, rinsed	125 mL
1 1/2 cups	diced peeled sweet potatoes	375 mL
1 1/2 cups	diced zucchini	375 mL
	Salt and pepper	

1. In a large Dutch oven or stockpot, melt butter over medium heat. Add onion, garlic, rutabaga and thyme; cook, stirring often, for 5 minutes or until vegetables are lightly colored.
2. Stir in stock and barley; bring to a boil. Reduce heat, cover and simmer for 20 minutes. Add sweet potatoes and zucchini; simmer, covered, for 15 minutes or until barley is tender. Season with salt and pepper to taste.

Per serving	
Calories	203
Protein	10 g
Carbohydrates	28 g
Dietary Fiber	5 g
Fat - Total	6 g
Saturated Fat	3 g
Calcium	55 mg

Cultivated mussels are the perfect fast food. They come debearded (meaning the thread that holds them to stationary objects has already been removed) and require only a quick rinse under cold water before cooking. Just throw them in a pot, steam for 4 to 5 minutes and they're ready to eat.

TIP

To store mussels, place in a bowl and cover with damp paper towels. Never keep in a closed plastic bag or the mussels will suffocate. Also never put in a sink full of water or they will drown. For maximum freshness, use within 2 days of purchase.

VARIATION

Turkey Chowder

Follow recipe as directed. Omit wine; use 2 cups (500 mL) turkey stock instead of mussel broth. Replace mussels with 1 1/2 cups (375 mL) diced cooked turkey or chicken.

Per serving (6)	
Calories	279
Protein	23 g
Carbohydrates	21 g
Dietary Fiber	1 g
Fat - Total	8 g
Saturated Fat	3.1 g
Calcium	135 mg

Hearty Mussel Chowder

2 lbs	cultivated mussels	1 kg
1 cup	white wine *or* water	250 mL
4	slices bacon, chopped	4
1	large leek, white and light green part only, chopped	1
2	stalks celery, chopped	2
1 1/2 cups	diced peeled potatoes	375 mL
1/2 tsp	salt	2 mL
1/4 tsp	pepper	1 mL
1/2 cup	diced red bell pepper	125 mL
2 tbsp	all-purpose flour	25 mL
1 1/2 cups	milk (or use part light cream)	375 mL
2 tbsp	finely chopped parsley	25 mL

1. Place mussels and wine in a large saucepan. Cover and place over high heat; bring to a boil. Steam for 4 minutes or just until shells open. Drain, reserving cooking liquid. Add enough water or stock to make 2 cups (500 mL) liquid. Remove mussel meat from shells and place in a bowl; discard any that do not open.

2. In large saucepan over medium heat, cook bacon, stirring often, for 4 minutes or until crisp. Remove with slotted spoon; drain on paper towels. Pour off all but 2 tsp (10 mL) fat in pan. Add leek and celery; cook, stirring, for 3 minutes or until softened. Add potatoes, reserved mussel broth, salt and pepper. Bring to a boil; reduce heat, cover and simmer for 15 minutes or until potatoes are tender. Stir in red pepper.

3. In a bowl, blend flour with 1/4 cup (50 mL) of the milk to make a smooth paste; add remaining milk. Stir into saucepan; bring to a boil and cook, stirring, until thickened. Add reserved mussels, bacon bits and parsley; cook 2 minutes or until piping hot.

A generous bowlful of this nourishing soup makes an ideal lunch or light supper. Just add some pita bread or whole grain crackers.

TIP

Tabasco is my preferred brand of hot pepper sauce, especially for tomato-based dishes.

Cold soups taste best when refrigerated overnight, giving the flavors a chance to blend. Always check the seasoning of a cold soup, however. Often you will need to add extra salt, pepper or hot pepper sauce.

Per serving	
Calories	130
Protein	8 g
Carbohydrates	24 g
Dietary Fiber	7 g
Fat - Total	1 g
Saturated Fat	0.2 g
Calcium	83 mg

Spicy Black Bean Gazpacho

1	red bell pepper, coarsely chopped	1
3	green onions, coarsely chopped	3
3	ripe tomatoes, coarsely chopped	3
1	large clove garlic, minced	1
1	can (19 oz [540 mL]) black beans, rinsed and drained	1
1	can (19 oz [540 mL]) tomato juice	1
2 tbsp	balsamic vinegar	25 mL
1 tbsp	red wine vinegar	15 mL
	Salt and pepper	
1/2 to 1 tsp	hot pepper sauce	2 to 5 mL
1/3 cup	chopped fresh coriander *or* parsley	75 mL
	Light sour cream *or* plain yogurt	

1. In a food processor, finely chop red pepper and green onions, using on-off turns; transfer to a large bowl. Add tomatoes to food processor; finely chop, using on-off turns. Add to pepper-onion mixture along with black beans and tomato juice. Add balsamic and red wine vinegars; season with salt, pepper and hot pepper sauce to taste. Cover and refrigerate for 4 hours, preferably overnight.

2. Add about 1/3 cup (75 mL) cold water to thin soup, if desired. Adjust seasoning with vinegars, salt, pepper and hot pepper sauce. Ladle into chilled bowls; sprinkle with coriander and top with a spoonful of sour cream.

Perfect Potato and Leek Soup

Watercress adds a vibrant color and nip to the classic combo of creamed potato and leek soup.

TIP

You can make this soup a day ahead and reheat until piping hot. It's also delicious served cold.

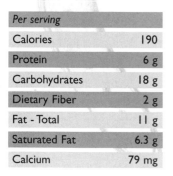

1 tbsp	butter	15 mL
2	medium leeks, white and light green part only, chopped	2
2 cups	diced peeled potatoes	500 mL
1 tsp	dried tarragon or *fines herbes*	5 mL
2 tbsp	all-purpose flour	25 mL
4 cups	chicken stock	1 L
1	bunch watercress, tough stems removed, chopped	1
1 cup	light (10%) cream or milk	250 mL
	Salt and pepper	
	Watercress sprigs	

1. In a large saucepan, melt butter over medium heat. Add leeks, potatoes and tarragon; cook, stirring, for 5 minutes or until leeks are softened but not browned. Blend in flour; stir in chicken stock. Bring to a boil; reduce heat, cover and simmer, stirring occasionally, for 20 minutes or until potatoes are very tender.

2. Add watercress; simmer 1 minute until watercress is limp and bright green in color. In a blender or food processor, purée soup in batches until smooth. Return to saucepan. Stir in cream; season with salt and pepper to taste. Heat until piping hot; do not let boil. Ladle into bowls; garnish with watercress sprigs.

Per serving	
Calories	190
Protein	6 g
Carbohydrates	18 g
Dietary Fiber	2 g
Fat - Total	11 g
Saturated Fat	6.3 g
Calcium	79 mg

SERVES 4

Gingery Squash Soup

Serve cupfuls of this colorful soup as an elegant starter to a fall menu. I turn to it when fresh-picked squash are plentiful in the market. I often make extra purée and freeze it in containers. It takes no time at all to make the soup if you have the purée on hand in the freezer. The finished soup also freezes well.

TIP

To make squash purée, cut I small butternut or large acorn squash (about 2 lbs [I kg]) into quarters; remove seeds. Place in large casserole dish with 1/2 cup (125 mL) water. Cover and microwave at High for 15 to 20 minutes or until squash is tender when pierced with a fork. (Cooking time varies with size and type of squash.) Let stand 15 minutes or until cool enough to handle. Scoop out pulp; place in food processor and purée. Makes about 2 cups (500 mL).

1 tbsp	butter	15 mL
1	large onion, chopped	1
2	cloves garlic, finely chopped	2
4 tsp	minced ginger root	20 mL
2 tbsp	all-purpose flour	25 mL
3 cups	chicken stock	750 mL
2 cups	cooked squash purée (such as butternut or acorn)	500 mL
1/2 cup	light (10%) cream or whipping (35%) cream	125 mL
1 tsp	grated orange zest	5 mL
	Salt, pepper and nutmeg	
2 tbsp	chopped fresh chives *or* parsley	25 mL

1. In a large saucepan, melt butter over medium-low heat. Add onion, garlic and ginger; cook, stirring often, for 5 minutes or until onion is softened. Blend in flour; stir in stock and squash. Bring to a boil and cook, stirring, until thickened. Reduce heat, cover and simmer for 10 minutes.

2. In a food processor or blender, purée in batches until smooth. Return to saucepan. Add cream and orange zest; season with salt, pepper and nutmeg to taste. Heat until piping hot. Ladle into bowls; sprinkle with chives.

Per serving	
Calories	193
Protein	7 g
Carbohydrates	21 g
Dietary Fiber	4 g
Fat - Total	10 g
Saturated Fat	5.7 g
Calcium	73 mg

Basil Tomato-Rice Soup

My pantry can be sparse, but I can always count on having these few ingredients on hand to make this last-minute soup to serve with crusty wholegrain bread and cheese.

TIP

Instead of canned tomatoes, use 4 large ripe tomatoes, peeled and chopped.

To make a creamy tomato-rice soup, add 1/2 cup (125 mL) whipping (35%) cream along with the parsley.

If you have fresh basil on hand, substitute 2 tbsp (25 mL) of the chopped fresh herb for the dried basil in recipe and add along with parsley.

1 tbsp	olive oil	15 mL
1	large onion, chopped	1
2	stalks celery, chopped	2
2	cloves garlic, finely chopped	2
1 tsp	dried basil	5 mL
1	can (28 oz [796 mL]) plum tomatoes, puréed	1
6 cups	chicken stock *or* vegetable stock	1.5 L
1/2 cup	long-grain white rice	125 mL
1 tsp	granulated sugar (approximate)	5 mL
	Salt and pepper	
2 tbsp	chopped parsley	25 mL

1. In a Dutch oven or stockpot, heat oil over medium heat. Add onion, celery, garlic and basil; cook, stirring, for 5 minutes or until softened.
2. Add tomatoes, stock and rice; season with sugar, salt and pepper to taste. Bring to a boil; reduce heat, cover and simmer for 30 to 35 minutes or until rice is tender. Stir in parsley.

Per serving	
Calories	165
Protein	8 g
Carbohydrates	25 g
Dietary Fiber	2 g
Fat - Total	4 g
Saturated Fat	0.8 g
Calcium	79 mg

Here's a homey satisfying soup that's perfect to serve as the main event on cold, blustery days.

TIP

This recipe makes a large batch of soup; freeze extra for another meal.

If you have any leftover baked ham, dice into small cubes and add along with the split peas. Another option is to add diced smoked sausage such as kielbasa for the last 15 minutes of cooking.

Curried Split-Pea Soup

1 tbsp	vegetable oil	15 mL
2	medium onions, chopped	2
4	cloves garlic, finely chopped	4
1 tbsp	curry powder	15 mL
1 tsp	ground cumin	5 mL
1 tsp	paprika	5 mL
1/4 tsp	cayenne pepper	1 mL
3	large carrots, peeled and chopped	3
2	large stalks celery with leaves, chopped	2
2 cups	yellow or green split peas, rinsed and sorted	500 mL
1/4 cup	tomato paste	50 mL
10 cups	vegetable stock *or* chicken stock	2.5 L
1/3 cup	chopped fresh coriander or parsley	75 mL
	Salt and pepper	
	Plain yogurt (optional)	

1. In a large Dutch oven or stockpot, heat oil over medium heat. Add onions, garlic, curry powder, cumin, paprika and cayenne pepper; cook, stirring, for 3 minutes or until softened.

2. Add carrots, celery, split peas, tomato paste and stock. Bring to a boil; reduce heat, cover and simmer for about 1 to 1 1/2 hours or until peas are tender.

3. Stir in coriander; season with salt and pepper to taste. Ladle into bowls; top with a dollop of yogurt, if desired. Soup thickens as it cools, so you may want to thin with additional stock before serving.

Per serving	
Calories	253
Protein	17 g
Carbohydrates	44 g
Dietary Fiber	2 g
Fat - Total	3 g
Saturated Fat	0.2 g
Calcium	30 mg

A POUND OF GROUND

MAKES 4 BURGERS

Mama's Italian Cheeseburgers

If burgers are starting to become mundane, put some excitement in those patties. Instead of cheese on top of the burger, put shredded cheese right in the ground meat mixture for moist burgers with a twist. Mama would be pleased.

TIP

For an easy vegetable topping, cut green or red bell peppers and a large red onion into rounds, brush lightly with olive oil and grill alongside burgers.

1/4 cup	tomato pasta sauce	50 mL
1/4 cup	grated or minced onion	50 mL
1	clove garlic, minced	1
1/4 tsp	dried basil or oregano	1 mL
1/4 tsp	salt	1 mL
1/4 tsp	pepper	1 mL
3/4 cup	shredded part-skim mozzarella or Fontina cheese	175 mL
1/3 cup	dry seasoned bread crumbs	75 mL
1 lb	lean ground beef	500 g
4	hamburger buns, split and lightly toasted	4

1. In a bowl combine tomato pasta sauce, onion, garlic, basil, salt and pepper. Stir in cheese and bread crumbs; mix in beef. Shape into four 3/4-inch (2 cm) thick patties.

2. Place on greased grill over medium-high heat; cook, turning once, for 6 to 7 minutes on each side, or until no longer pink in center. Serve in buns.

Per burger	
Calories	469
Protein	32 g
Carbohydrates	31 g
Dietary Fiber	2 g
Fat - Total	24 g
Saturated Fat	9.6 g
Calcium	225 mg

SERVES 4

Middle Eastern Lamb Burgers

PREHEAT BARBECUE GRILL OR BROILER

I love the combination of spices and dried fruits in Middle Eastern cooking. Here, the cucumber-yogurt relish offers a cool counterpoint to richly spiced burgers, which can be tucked into pita bread pockets or crusty Kaiser rolls.

TIP

If ground lamb is unavailable, use lean ground beef or turkey instead.

Cucumber-Yogurt Relish

1 cup	finely diced seedless cucumber	250 mL
1 cup	plain low-fat yogurt	250 mL
2 tbsp	chopped fresh mint *or* coriander *or* chives	25 mL
1	small clove garlic, minced	1
	Salt	

Burgers

1	egg	1
1/3 cup	finely chopped green onions	75 mL
1/4 cup	raisins	50 mL
2 tbsp	fine dry bread crumbs	25 mL
1/2 tsp	ground cumin	2 mL
1/2 tsp	ground coriander	2 mL
1/2 tsp	salt	2 mL
1/2 tsp	pepper	2 mL
Pinch	cinnamon	Pinch
1 lb	lean ground lamb	500 g
4	pita breads (7-inch [18 cm] size), halved to make pockets	4

1. Cucumber-Yogurt Relish: In a bowl combine cucumber, yogurt, mint and garlic. Season with salt to taste.

2. Burgers: In a bowl, beat egg; stir in green onions, raisins, bread crumbs, cumin, coriander, salt, pepper and cinnamon. Mix in ground lamb. Shape into four 1/2-inch (1 cm) thick patties.

3. Place on greased grill over medium heat; cook 5 to 6 minutes on each side or until no longer pink in center. Wrap pita breads in foil; place on grill for 10 minutes, turning once, until heated through. (Or wrap in paper towels; microwave at Medium for 1 1/2 minutes or until warm.) Cut burgers into halves; place in pita pockets. Top with Cucumber-Yogurt Relish.

Per burger	
Calories	497
Protein	31 g
Carbohydrates	51 g
Dietary Fiber	3 g
Fat - Total	19 g
Saturated Fat	8.3 g
Calcium	213 mg

Go beyond the standard backyard burger with these boldly spiced patties served with a fresh salsa. They are great to serve for company. Tuck the sliced meat into pita pockets or flour tortillas for sandwich wraps.

TIP

To make soft bread crumbs, process 2 slices white or whole wheat sandwich bread in a food processor to make fine crumbs.

Chili Burgers in Pita Pockets

PREHEAT BARBECUE GRILL OR BROILER

1	egg	1
1	large clove garlic, minced	1
1 cup	soft bread crumbs	250 mL
1/4 cup	finely chopped parsley	50 mL
1 tsp	chili powder	5 mL
1/2 tsp	dried oregano	2 mL
1/2 tsp	salt	2 mL
1/2 tsp	pepper	2 mL
12 oz	lean ground beef	375 g
12 oz	lean ground pork or veal	375 g
6	pita breads (7-inch [18 cm] size), halved to make pockets	6
	Lettuce leaves	
	Light sour cream or yogurt	
	TOMATO-PEPPER SALSA (see recipe, page 57) *or* bottled salsa	

1. In a bowl, beat egg; stir in garlic, bread crumbs, parsley, chili powder, oregano, salt and pepper. Mix in beef and pork. Shape into 3 patties, each 5 inches (12 cm) in diameter.

2. Place on greased grill over medium heat; cook for 8 to 10 minutes on each side or until no longer pink in center. (Or place under preheated broiler, 5 inches [12 cm] from heat, for 8 to 10 minutes on each side or until no longer pink in center.) Transfer to a cutting board; let rest 5 minutes for easy slicing. Cut into thin slices.

3. Wrap pita breads in foil; place on grill for about 10 minutes, turning once until heated through. (Or wrap in paper towels; microwave at Medium for 2 minutes or until warm.) Line pita breads with lettuce; tuck in meat slices. Top with sour cream and TOMATO-PEPPER SALSA.

Per serving	
Calories	403
Protein	28 g
Carbohydrates	37 g
Dietary Fiber	1 g
Fat - Total	15 g
Saturated Fat	5.3 g
Calcium	76 mg

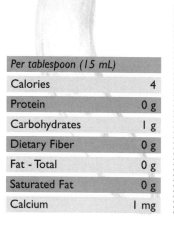

Serve this versatile fresh condiment with grilled favorites such as fish and chicken. It's best served the same day it's made.

Tomato-Pepper Salsa

2	ripe tomatoes, seeded and diced	2
1	yellow or green bell pepper, finely diced	1
2	green onions, finely chopped	2
1 tbsp	freshly squeezed lime juice *or* lemon juice	15 mL
1/4 tsp	ground cumin	1 mL
	Salt, pepper and hot pepper sauce	

1. In a bowl, combine tomatoes, bell pepper, green onions, lime juice and cumin; season with salt, pepper and a generous amount of hot pepper sauce to taste. Refrigerate until ready to use.

Per tablespoon (15 mL)	
Calories	4
Protein	0 g
Carbohydrates	1 g
Dietary Fiber	0 g
Fat - Total	0 g
Saturated Fat	0 g
Calcium	1 mg

Here's a satisfying meat loaf-like dish with a tasty gravy that's wonderful with creamy mashed potatoes. Peel the potatoes and start them cooking on the stovetop before you begin preparing the patties so both will be ready at about the same time.

TIP

Put tablespoons (15 mL) of leftover canned tomato paste on a waxed paper-lined plate or in ice-cube trays; freeze until firm. Transfer to a small freezer bag and have handy in the freezer to add to recipes.

Swift 'n' Savory Beef Patties

1	egg	1
2 tbsp	fine dry bread crumbs	25 mL
1	small onion, minced	1
1 tbsp	Worcestershire sauce	15 mL
1/2 tsp	salt	2 mL
1/4 tsp	pepper	1 mL
1 lb	lean ground beef	500 g
2 tsp	vegetable oil	10 mL
1 1/2 cups	chopped mushrooms	375 mL
1	clove garlic, minced	1
1/4 tsp	dried thyme or marjoram	1 mL
1 tbsp	all-purpose flour	15 mL
1 cup	beef stock	250 mL
1 tbsp	tomato paste	15 mL

1. In a bowl, beat egg; stir in bread crumbs, half the onion, half the Worcestershire sauce, salt and pepper; mix in ground beef. Form into 4 patties, each 4 inches (10 cm) in diameter.

2. In a large nonstick skillet, heat oil over medium-high heat; brown patties, about 2 minutes on each side. Transfer to a plate. Add remaining onion, mushrooms, garlic and thyme to skillet; cook, stirring, for 2 minutes or until softened.

3. Sprinkle with flour; stir in remaining Worcestershire sauce, beef stock and tomato paste. Cook, stirring, for 1 minute or until thickened. Return patties to skillet; reduce heat, cover and simmer, turning once, for 10 minutes or until patties are no longer pink in center.

Per serving	
Calories	328
Protein	25 g
Carbohydrates	8 g
Dietary Fiber	1 g
Fat - Total	21 g
Saturated Fat	7.5 g
Calcium	40 mg

Mini Veal Meat Loaves

Ground meats are one of the best supermarket buys for budget-trimming meals. I serve these mini meat loaves with fluffy mashed potatoes and balsamic-glazed carrots for a delicious, economical supper.

TIP

Instead of canned chicken stock, use 1 chicken stock cube dissolved in 1/2 cup (125 mL) water.

PREHEAT OVEN TO 400° F (200° C)
UNGREASED MUFFIN PAN

1/2 cup	undiluted canned chicken stock	125 mL
1	medium onion, finely chopped	1
1	large clove garlic, minced	1
1/2 tsp	dried thyme, marjoram or basil	2 mL
1/4 tsp	pepper	1 mL
1/2 cup	dry seasoned bread crumbs	125 mL
1/4 cup	finely chopped parsley	50 mL
1 tsp	grated lemon zest	5 mL
1 1/2 lbs	lean ground veal or beef	750 g
1	egg, beaten	1

1. In a large microwave-safe bowl, combine stock, onion, garlic, thyme and pepper. Microwave at High for 2 minutes or until onion is tender. Stir in bread crumbs, parsley and lemon zest; mix in ground veal and egg.

2. Divide into 12 balls; lightly press into muffin cups. Bake for 20 minutes or until no longer pink in center. Drain off juice.

Per serving (2 mini meat loaves)	
Calories	180
Protein	20 g
Carbohydrates	9 g
Dietary Fiber	1 g
Fat - Total	7 g
Saturated Fat	2.5 g
Calcium	48 mg

**MAKES 48 MEATBALLS
SERVES 6 AS
A MAIN COURSE OR
8 AS AN APPETIZER**

Take advantage of supermarket specials for lean ground beef and cook batches of meatballs ahead. Freeze them for this quick dish.

TIP

Place cooked meatballs in a single layer on a rimmed baking sheet and freeze. Transfer to a covered container or freezer bag. To reheat, place frozen meatballs in a casserole dish, cover and microwave at Medium until defrosted.

Per serving (8)	
Calories	276
Protein	18 g
Carbohydrates	19 g
Dietary Fiber	1 g
Fat - Total	14 g
Saturated Fat	5.4 g
Calcium	36 mg

Everyone's Favorite Sweet-and-Sour Meatballs

**PREHEAT OVEN TO 400° F (200° C)
RIMMED BAKING SHEET**

Meatballs

1	egg	1
1 tbsp	soya sauce	15 mL
3	green onions, finely chopped	3
1	large clove garlic, minced	1
1/3 cup	fine dry bread crumbs	75 mL
1 1/2 lbs	lean ground beef	750 g

Sauce

1	can (14 oz [398 mL]) pineapple chunks, drained, juice reserved	1
1/4 cup	packed brown sugar	50 mL
1/4 cup	rice vinegar	50 mL
1/4 cup	soya sauce	50 mL
4 tsp	cornstarch	20 mL

1. Meatballs: In a large bowl, beat egg; stir in 1 tbsp (15 mL) water, soya sauce, green onions and garlic. Mix in bread crumbs and beef. With wet hands, form into 1-inch (2.5 cm) meatballs; arrange on a baking sheet. Bake for 15 minutes or until browned and no longer pink in center. Drain on paper towels.

2. Sauce: Pour pineapple juice into a measuring cup and add enough water to make 1 cup (250 mL). In a large saucepan, stir together pineapple juice, brown sugar, vinegar, soya sauce and cornstarch until smooth. Place over medium heat and cook, stirring, until sauce comes to a boil and thickens. Stir in meatballs and pineapple chunks; cook for 3 to 5 minutes or until piping hot.

MAKES 5 PATTIES

Terrific Turkey Patties

Layer these patties in a toasted onion bun for an easy burger supper or accompany them with stir-fried rice and vegetables.

TIP

Turkey can be easily substituted for beef in other burger recipes. Since turkey is moister, use 1/3 to 1/2 cup (75 to 125 mL) dry bread crumbs to the meat mixture so patties don't fall apart.

1	egg	1
1/2 cup	fine dry bread crumbs	125 mL
1/3 cup	finely chopped green onions	75 mL
1 tsp	ground coriander	5 mL
1 tsp	grated lemon zest	5 mL
1/2 tsp	salt	2 mL
1/4 tsp	pepper	1 mL
1 lb	ground turkey or chicken	500 g
2 tsp	vegetable oil	10 mL

1. In a bowl, beat egg; add bread crumbs, green onions, coriander, lemon zest, salt and pepper. Mix in chicken; with wet hands, shape into 5 patties, each 4 inches (10 cm) in diameter.

2. In a large nonstick skillet, heat oil over medium heat; cook patties for 5 to 6 minutes on each side or until golden brown on outside and no longer pink in center.

Per patty	
Calories	213
Protein	19 g
Carbohydrates	9 g
Dietary Fiber	1 g
Fat - Total	11 g
Saturated Fat	2.8 g
Calcium	44 mg

Leftover pasta in the fridge is perfect for this pizza-like supper dish that's especially appealing to the younger set.

TIP

It's easy to turn this recipe into a vegetarian dish – just omit the meat.

Broccoli can be replaced by zucchini, bell peppers or whatever vegetables you have on hand.

Kids' Favorite Spaghetti Pie

PREHEAT OVEN TO 350° F (180° C)
9- OR 10-INCH (23 OR 25 CM) GLASS PIE PLATE, OILED

8 oz	mild or hot Italian sausages, casings removed *or* lean ground beef	250 g
2 cups	sliced mushrooms	500 mL
1	small onion, chopped	1
1	large clove garlic, finely chopped	1
1 1/2 tsp	dried oregano	7 mL
2 cups	tomato pasta sauce	500 mL
2 cups	small broccoli florets	500 mL
3 cups	cooked spaghetti or other string pasta (6 oz [175 g] uncooked)	750 mL
1 1/2 cups	shredded part-skim mozzarella cheese	375 mL

1. In a medium saucepan over medium-high heat, cook sausage meat, breaking up with a wooden spoon, for 4 minutes or until no longer pink. Drain in sieve to remove any fat. Return to saucepan. Add mushrooms, onion, garlic, and oregano; cook, stirring, for 3 minutes or until vegetables are softened. Add tomato pasta sauce; cover and simmer for 10 minutes.

2. Rinse broccoli; place in a covered casserole dish. Microwave at High for 2 to 2 1/2 minutes or until bright green and almost tender. Rinse under cold water to chill; drain.

3. Arrange spaghetti in pie plate. Spread with meat sauce; top with broccoli and sprinkle with cheese. Bake for 25 to 30 minutes or until cheese is melted. Cut into wedges and serve.

Per serving	
Calories	487
Protein	30 g
Carbohydrates	53 g
Dietary Fiber	4 g
Fat - Total	19 g
Saturated Fat	7.6 g
Calcium	351 mg

Fast Italian Skillet Supper

No need to buy pricey packaged dinner mixes when it's easy to create your own. It's just a matter of using pantry staples already in your cupboard. In about the time it takes to fix an accompanying salad, this dish is ready to set on the table.

TIP

Use your own homemade tomato sauce or rely on the many top-notch bottled sauces now available in supermarkets to cut down on preparation time.

1 lb	lean ground beef *or* turkey	500 g
1	small onion, chopped	1
2	cloves garlic, finely chopped	2
1 tsp	dried basil *or* oregano	5 mL
1 1/2 cups	tomato pasta sauce	375 mL
1 1/2 cups	chicken stock *or* beef stock (approximate)	375 mL
1 cup	elbow macaroni	250 mL
2	medium zucchini, cut into 1/2-inch (1 cm) cubes	2

1. In a large nonstick skillet over medium-high heat, cook ground beef, breaking up with a wooden spoon, for 5 minutes or until no longer pink. Add onion, garlic and basil; cook, stirring, for 2 minutes.

2. Add tomato pasta sauce and stock; bring to a boil. Stir in pasta; reduce heat, cover and cook for 5 minutes. Stir in zucchini; cook, covered, stirring occasionally, adding more stock if needed, for 5 to 7 minutes or until pasta and zucchini are tender.

Per serving	
Calories	437
Protein	29 g
Carbohydrates	33 g
Dietary Fiber	2 g
Fat - Total	21 g
Saturated Fat	7.5 g
Calcium	54 mg

SERVES 4

Quick Chicken Paprika with Noodles

Economical ground meats provide versatile options for the harried cook. Serve this tasty ground chicken dish with a salad or green vegetable such as broccoli. Dinner is ready in about 30 minutes.

TIP

When ground chicken is browned in a skillet, it doesn't turn into a fine crumble like other ground meats. I overcome the problem by placing the cooked chicken in a food processor and chopping it using on-off turns to break up meat lumps.

1 lb	ground chicken or turkey	500 g
1 tbsp	butter	15 mL
1	medium onion, chopped	1
8 oz	mushrooms, sliced	250 g
1 tbsp	sweet Hungarian paprika	15 mL
2 tbsp	all-purpose flour	25 mL
1 1/3 cups	chicken stock	325 mL
1/2 cup	light sour cream	125 mL
2 tbsp	chopped fresh dill *or* parsley	25 mL
	Salt and pepper	
8 oz	fettuccine *or* broad egg noodles	250 g

1. In a large nonstick skillet over medium-high heat, cook chicken, breaking up with a wooden spoon, for 5 minutes or until no longer pink. Remove; drain in sieve to remove any fat and set aside.

2. Melt butter in skillet. Add onion, mushrooms and paprika; cook, stirring often, for 3 minutes or until vegetables are softened.

3. Sprinkle with flour; stir in stock and return chicken to skillet. Bring to a boil; cook, stirring, until thickened. Reduce heat, cover and simmer for 5 minutes. Remove from heat and stir in sour cream (it may curdle if added over the heat) and dill; season with salt and pepper to taste.

4. Cook pasta in a large pot of boiling salted water until tender but firm. Drain well. Return to pot and toss with chicken mixture. Serve immediately.

Per serving	
Calories	563
Protein	33 g
Carbohydrates	55 g
Dietary Fiber	6 g
Fat - Total	23 g
Saturated Fat	4.1 g
Calcium	90 mg

MAMA'S ITALIAN CHEESEBURGERS (PAGE 54)
OVERLEAF: SIMPLY SUPER SALMON WITH LEMON-OREGANO PESTO (PAGE 109)

SERVES 6

Beefy Macaroni with Cabbage

Here's a pasta dish with all the appeal of cabbage rolls, but is far easier to whip up for dinner. Its sweet-sour accent is a welcome departure from traditional pasta sauces and a good match for the cabbage.

TIP

The dish can be made a day ahead and reheated; it also freezes well. As a time-saver, buy packaged shredded cabbage in the produce department.

1 lb	lean ground beef	500 g
1	large onion, chopped	1
2	large cloves garlic, minced	2
1/2 tsp	fennel seeds	2 mL
8 cups	shredded cabbage (1 lb [500 g] pkg)	2 L
2 tbsp	red wine vinegar	25 mL
2 tbsp	brown sugar	25 mL
1	can (28 oz [796 mL]) stewed tomatoes	1
1 tsp	salt	5 mL
1/2 tsp	pepper	2 mL
2 cups	elbow macaroni	500 mL

1. In a Dutch oven or large saucepan over high heat, cook beef, breaking up with a wooden spoon, for 5 minutes or until no longer pink.

2. Reduce heat to medium. Add onion, garlic and fennel seeds; cook, stirring often, for 3 minutes or until onion is softened. Stir in cabbage, vinegar and brown sugar; cook, stirring often, for 3 minutes or until cabbage is wilted. Stir in stewed tomatoes, salt and pepper. Bring to a boil; reduce heat, cover and simmer for 5 minutes or until cabbage is tender.

3. Meanwhile, cook pasta in a large pot of boiling salted water until tender but firm. Drain well. Stir into cabbage mixture; cook for 2 minutes or until piping hot.

Per serving	
Calories	380
Protein	21 g
Carbohydrates	47 g
Dietary Fiber	6 g
Fat - Total	13 g
Saturated Fat	4.7 g
Calcium	101 mg

◄ MAKE-AHEAD SOUTHWESTERN PORK STEW (PAGE 81)

Looking for an inviting dinner-in-a-dish everyone in the family will enjoy? This hearty chili-flavored beef casserole topped with a tasty cornbread crust fills the bill. I've kept the seasonings tame so it appeals to the sensitive taste buds of young diners, but boost the seasonings if desired.

TIP

Add 1 tsp (5 mL) additional chili powder along with 1/4 tsp (1 mL) red pepper flakes or to taste, to the ground beef mixture for a more assertive chili flavor.

Per serving (6)	
Calories	419
Protein	24 g
Carbohydrates	42 g
Dietary Fiber	4 g
Fat - Total	17 g
Saturated Fat	7.4 g
Calcium	140 mg

Tex-Mex Beef Cobbler with Cheddar Cornbread

PREHEAT OVEN TO 400° F (200° C)
10-CUP (2.5 L) CASSEROLE DISH

1 lb	lean ground beef	500 g
1	onion, chopped	1
2	cloves garlic, finely chopped	2
1	large green bell pepper, chopped	1
2 tsp	chili powder	10 mL
1 tsp	dried oregano	5 mL
1/2 tsp	ground cumin	2 mL
2 tbsp	all-purpose flour	25 mL
1 1/2 cups	beef stock	375 mL
1	can (7 1/2 oz [213 mL]) tomato sauce	1
1	can (12 oz [341 mL]) corn kernels, drained	1

Cheddar Cornbread

2/3 cup	all-purpose flour	150 mL
1/2 cup	cornmeal	125 mL
1 1/2 tsp	granulated sugar	7 mL
1 1/2 tsp	baking powder	7 mL
1/4 tsp	salt	1 mL
1/2 cup	shredded Cheddar cheese	125 mL
1	large egg	1
2/3 cup	milk	150 mL

1. In a large nonstick skillet over medium-high heat, cook beef, breaking up with a wooden spoon, for 5 minutes or until no longer pink. Stir in onion, garlic, green pepper, chili powder, oregano and cumin; cook, stirring, for 4 minutes or until softened. Blend in flour; stir in stock and tomato sauce. Bring to a boil, stirring, until thickened. Reduce heat, cover and simmer for 5 minutes. Stir in corn; cook for 2 minutes or until piping hot. Spoon into casserole dish.

2. Cornbread: In a bowl combine flour, cornmeal, sugar, baking powder and salt; mix in cheese. In another bowl, beat together egg and milk. Stir into dry ingredients to make a smooth batter. Spoon over beef mixture in an even layer. Bake for 20 to 25 minutes or until top is light golden and filling is bubbly.

Looking for a fast-track dinner? Convenient frozen hash browns come to the rescue along with quick-cooking ground beef for a family-pleasing meal.

TIP

To defrost hash browns, place on plate lined with paper towels; microwave at High for 3 to 4 minutes, stirring once.

VARIATION

Breakfast Sausage and Potato Hash with Poached Eggs
Substitute breakfast sausage (with casings removed) for the beef. Prepare recipe as directed; omit Worcestershire sauce. Divide mixture among 4 serving plates and top each with a poached or fried egg.

In-a-Hurry Beef and Potato Hash

1 lb	lean ground beef	500 g
2 tsp	Worcestershire sauce	10 mL
1 tbsp	vegetable oil	15 mL
1	medium onion, chopped	1
1	green bell pepper, chopped	1
4 cups	frozen hash brown potatoes, defrosted	1 L
	Salt and pepper	

1. In a large nonstick skillet over medium-high heat, cook beef, breaking up with a wooden spoon, for 5 minutes or until no longer pink. Place in sieve to drain any fat; transfer to a bowl. Stir in Worcestershire sauce.

2. Add oil to skillet; cook onion, green pepper and potatoes, stirring often, for 8 to 10 minutes or until potatoes are golden. Add ground beef; season with salt and pepper to taste. Cook for 2 minutes or until heated through.

Per serving	
Calories	464
Protein	26 g
Carbohydrates	41 g
Dietary Fiber	4 g
Fat - Total	22 g
Saturated Fat	7.4 g
Calcium	39 mg

Here's a streamlined version of chili that's a snap. Make a double batch and have containers stashed away in the freezer for quick microwave meals. Just ladle into bowls and, if desired, top with shredded Monterey Jack cheese. Set out a basket of crusty bread — supper is that easy.

TIP

Add just a pinch of red pepper flakes for a mild chili; but if you want to turn up the heat, use amount specified in the recipe.

20-Minute Chili

1 lb	lean ground beef *or* turkey	500 g
1	large onion, chopped	1
2	large cloves garlic, finely chopped	2
1	large green bell pepper, chopped	1
4 tsp	chili powder	20 mL
1 tbsp	all-purpose flour	15 mL
1 tsp	dried basil	5 mL
1 tsp	dried oregano	5 mL
1/4 to 1/2 tsp	red pepper flakes	1 to 2 mL
2 cups	tomato pasta sauce	500 mL
1 1/3 cups	beef stock	325 mL
1	can (19 oz [540 mL]) kidney beans *or* pinto beans, rinsed and drained	1
	Salt and pepper	

1. In a Dutch oven or large saucepan over medium-high heat, cook beef, breaking up with a wooden spoon, for 5 minutes or until no longer pink.
2. Reduce heat to medium. Add onion, garlic, green pepper, chili powder, flour, basil, oregano and red pepper flakes; cook, stirring, for 4 minutes or until vegetables are softened. Stir in tomato sauce and stock. Bring to a boil; cook, stirring, until thickened. Add beans; season with salt and pepper to taste. Reduce heat and simmer, covered, for 10 minutes.

Per serving (6)	
Calories	351
Protein	23 g
Carbohydrates	33 g
Dietary Fiber	9 g
Fat - Total	15 g
Saturated Fat	5.1 g
Calcium	49 mg

Some days you just don't have time to think about what's for supper. Rather than getting takeout, here's an easy dish that counts on convenient frozen vegetables to get dinner on the table in 20 minutes.

TIP

Cook extra rice ahead and keep it handy in the fridge. Or use instant rice prepared according to package directions.

Speedy Beef and Vegetable Fried Rice

1 lb	lean ground beef	500 g
3	green onions, chopped	3
1	large clove garlic, minced	1
2 tsp	minced ginger root (or 1/2 tsp [2 mL] ground ginger)	10 mL
2 cups	cooked rice, preferably basmati	500 mL
4 cups	frozen Oriental mixed vegetables	1 L
3 tbsp	soya sauce	45 mL

1. In a large nonstick skillet over high heat, cook beef, breaking up with a wooden spoon, for 5 minutes or until no longer pink. Add green onions, garlic and ginger; cook, stirring, for 1 minute. Stir in rice; cook, stirring, for 2 minutes.

2. Add vegetables and soya sauce. Reduce heat to medium, cover and cook, stirring occasionally (adding 2 tbsp [25 mL] water if necessary to prevent from sticking), for 5 minutes or until vegetables are tender.

Per serving	
Calories	430
Protein	25 g
Carbohydrates	35 g
Dietary Fiber	2 g
Fat - Total	20 g
Saturated Fat	7.3 g
Calcium	34 mg

Salsa Beef and Rice Casserole

Here's a terrific make-ahead casserole dish that reheats in the microwave in about the same time as it takes to toss a salad and set the table.

TIP

To oven-bake, cover and place in a 375° F (190° C) oven for 40 minutes; remove cover and bake another 15 to 20 minutes or until center is piping hot and cheese is golden.

Replace half or all the beef with Italian sausages. Remove casings and brown sausage meat; drain well.

To cook rice, bring 2 cups (500 mL) water to a boil in a medium saucpan; add 1 cup (250 mL) white long grain rice and 1/2 tsp (2 mL) salt. Return to a boil; reduce heat to low, cover and simmer for 20 minutes. If using brown rice, increase water to 2 1/2 cups (625 mL) and increase cooking time to 40 to 45 minutes. Makes 3 cups (750 mL) rice.

Per serving (6)	
Calories	431
Protein	24 g
Carbohydrates	40 g
Dietary Fiber	4 g
Fat - Total	20 g
Saturated Fat	8.9 g
Calcium	62 mg

10-CUP (2.5 L) CASSEROLE DISH

2 tsp	vegetable oil	10 mL
2	medium zucchini, halved lengthwise, thinly sliced	2
1 1/2 cups	fresh, frozen or canned corn kermels	375 mL
1 1/2 cups	medium salsa	375 mL
1 lb	lean ground beef	500 g
1	medium onion, finely chopped	1
2	large cloves garlic, minced	2
4 tsp	chili powder	20 mL
1 tsp	dried oregano	5 mL
1 tsp	salt	5 mL
1/2 tsp	pepper	2 mL
3 cups	cooked white or brown rice	750 mL
1 cup	shredded Cheddar cheese	250 mL

1. In a large nonstick skillet, heat oil over medium-high heat. Add zucchini and cook, stirring, for 3 minutes or until softened. Transfer to a bowl; stir in corn and salsa.

2. Add beef to skillet; cook, breaking up with a wooden spoon, for 5 minutes or until no longer pink. Add onion, garlic, chili powder, oregano, salt and pepper; cook, stirring, for 3 minutes. Stir in rice.

3. In a casserole dish, layer half the beef mixture, then half the vegetable mixture. Repeat layers. Sprinkle with cheese. Cover and microwave at High for 12 to 16 minutes (5 to 7 minutes longer if refrigerated) or until piping hot in center.

SERVES 4 TO 5

Everyone loves meat loaf and mashed potatoes. Here's a creative way to prepare this favorite combo.

TIP

Make a double batch of meatloaf. Press into 2 pie plates; bake according to recipe until no longer pink in center. Top one meatloaf with mashed potatoes; let the other one cool, wrap well and freeze for another meal.

Per serving (5)	
Calories	467
Protein	27 g
Carbohydrates	43 g
Dietary Fiber	3 g
Fat - Total	21 g
Saturated Fat	9.9 g
Calcium	113 mg

Meat Loaf and Mashed Potato Pie

PREHEAT OVEN TO 375° F (190° C)
DEEP 9- OR 10-INCH (23 OR 25 CM) PIE PLATE, OILED

2 lbs	russet or Yukon Gold potatoes, peeled and cubed	1 kg
1/2 cup	light sour cream (approximate)	125 mL
	Salt and pepper	

Meat loaf

1	egg	1
1/4 cup	bottled chili sauce *or* ketchup	50 mL
1/4 cup	minced onion	50 mL
1	clove garlic, minced	1
1 tsp	Worcestershire sauce	5 mL
1/2 tsp	salt	2 mL
1/4 tsp	pepper	1 mL
1/4 cup	dry seasoned bread crumbs	50 mL
1 lb	lean ground beef or veal	500 g
1/2 cup	shredded Cheddar cheese	125 mL

1. In a large saucepan, cook potatoes in boiling salted water until tender. Drain well and return to saucepan; place over low heat for 1 minute to dry. Mash using potato masher or electric mixer at low speed until smooth. Beat in sour cream; season with salt and pepper to taste. Keep warm over low heat.

2. Meat loaf: In a bowl, beat egg; stir in chili sauce, onion, garlic, Worcestershire sauce, salt and pepper. Mix in bread crumbs and beef. Press evenly in pie plate. Bake for 25 to 30 minutes or until no longer pink in center; drain off juice.

3. Spread mashed potatoes over meat; sprinkle with cheese. (Can be prepared up to 1 day ahead; cover and refrigerate.) Bake for 20 to 25 minutes or until cheese is melted. (Bake 10 minutes longer, if refrigerated.)

STEWS, CASSEROLES & ONE-POT SIMMERS

Everyone's Favorite Chicken Cacciatore

SERVES 4 TO 5

To survive the 6 o'clock week-night rush, batch-cook stews and sauce-based meals on weekends and keep in fridge for up to 3 days or freeze for easy reheating. When you breeze through the door at night, you simply have to decide whether you'll serve the stew with pasta or rice — and dinner's on the table.

TIP

One of the more popular poultry items now in supermarkets are skinless chicken thighs. They come with or without the bone and are a wonderfully economical alternative to more expensive chicken breasts.

3 tbsp	all-purpose flour	45 mL
1/2 tsp	salt	2 mL
1/2 tsp	pepper	2 mL
2 lbs	skinless chicken thighs	1 kg
2 tbsp	olive oil	25 mL
1	small onion, chopped	1
2	cloves garlic, finely chopped	2
3 cups	sliced mushrooms	750 mL
1/2 cup	white wine *or* chicken stock	125 mL
1	can (19 oz [540 mL]) tomatoes, chopped	1
1/3 cup	chopped sun-dried tomatoes	75 mL
1/4 cup	chopped fresh basil *or* parsley *or* a mixture of both	50 mL

1. In a heavy plastic bag, shake together flour, salt and pepper. In batches, toss chicken to coat, shaking off excess.

2. In a large Dutch oven, heat half the oil over medium-high heat. Brown chicken on all sides. Remove to a plate. Add remaining oil; cook onion, garlic and mushrooms, stirring, for 5 minutes or until softened.

3. Add wine; return chicken and any juices to pan along with canned and sun-dried tomatoes. Bring to a boil; reduce heat, cover and simmer for 35 minutes or until chicken is tender. Stir in basil; season with salt and pepper to taste.

Per serving (5)	
Calories	291
Protein	27 g
Carbohydrates	14 g
Dietary Fiber	3 g
Fat - Total	13 g
Saturated Fat	2.5 g
Calcium	52 mg

Caribbean Chicken Stew

Economical chicken thighs are perfect for hearty weeknight suppers. Here they star in a full-bodied stew with chunks of wholesome sweet potatoes. It's equally good when made with winter squash, such as butternut, instead of the potatoes.

TIP

If you plan to freeze this dish, cook the chicken, but do not add the sweet potatoes. When ready to complete cooking, let defrost overnight in the refrigerator or microwave at Medium, stirring occasionally. Then add the sweet potatoes and cook as directed in the recipe.

Sweet potatoes can be replaced with 4 medium potatoes, peeled and cubed, and 4 sliced carrots.

3 tbsp	all-purpose flour	45 mL
1/2 tsp	salt	2 mL
1/2 tsp	pepper	2 mL
2 lbs	skinless chicken thighs	1 kg
2 tbsp	vegetable oil	25 mL
1	large onion, chopped	1
2	cloves garlic, finely chopped	2
1 1/2 tsp	curry powder	7 mL
1 tsp	dried thyme	5 mL
1/2 tsp	dried marjoram	2 mL
1/4 tsp	red pepper flakes	1 mL
1 1/2 cups	chicken stock	375 mL
3	sweet potatoes, peeled and cut into 2-inch (5 cm) chunks	3
1/4 cup	chopped fresh coriander *or* parsley	50 mL

1. In a heavy plastic bag, shake together flour, salt and pepper. In batches, add chicken; shake to coat. In a large Dutch oven, heat half the oil over medium-high heat; brown chicken on all sides. Transfer to a plate.
2. Add remaining oil to pan. Reduce heat to medium. Add onion, garlic, curry powder, thyme, marjoram and red pepper flakes; cook, stirring, for 5 minutes or until vegetables are softened.
3. Add stock; bring to a boil. Return chicken and any juices to pan; cover and simmer for 20 minutes. (Dish can be frozen at this point.) Add sweet potatoes to pan; simmer, covered, for 20 minutes or until tender. Stir in coriander.

Per serving (5)	
Calories	355
Protein	28 g
Carbohydrates	30 g
Dietary Fiber	3 g
Fat - Total	13 g
Saturated Fat	2.3 g
Calcium	44 mg

SERVES 4

Even if you don't have a lot of time to spend in the kitchen, you can rustle up a great-tasting stew using boneless chicken thighs and convenient frozen vegetables. This satisfying dish does away with browning the chicken. You'll save time but not lose any flavor. Serve over noodles.

TIP

Use 5 cups (1.25 L) fresh vegetables instead of frozen, if you wish. Cut them into bite-sized pieces. For longer-cooking vegetables like carrots and celery, add them along with the chicken. For faster-cooking ones, such broccoli and zucchini, add in the last 10 minutes of cooking.

Streamlined Chicken and Vegetable Stew

1 tbsp	butter	15 mL
1	large onion, chopped	1
2	cloves garlic, finely chopped	2
1 tsp	dried Italian herbs or *fines herbes*	5 mL
8	skinless, boneless chicken thighs (about 1 lb [500 g]) cut into 1-inch (2.5 cm) cubes	8
3 tbsp	all-purpose flour	45 mL
2 cups	chicken stock	500 mL
1	pkg (1 lb [500 g]) frozen mixed vegetables	1
	Salt and pepper	

1. In a Dutch oven or large saucepan, melt butter over medium heat. Add onion, garlic and Italian herbs; cook, stirring, for 4 minutes or until lightly colored.

2. In a bowl toss chicken with flour until well-coated. Add to pan along with any remaining flour; stir in chicken stock. Bring to a boil and cook, stirring, until sauce thickens. Reduce heat, cover and simmer, stirring occasionally, for 20 minutes.

3. Add frozen vegetables; return to a boil. Season with salt and pepper to taste. Reduce heat, cover and simmer for 10 minutes or until chicken and vegetables are tender.

Per serving	
Calories	311
Protein	31 g
Carbohydrates	23 g
Dietary Fiber	6 g
Fat - Total	11 g
Saturated Fat	3.8 g
Calcium	49 mg

Instead of turning turkey left-overs into a week's worth of cold sandwiches, whip up this fast-fix dinner with loads of family appeal.

TIP

You can assemble this dish a day ahead of baking; just top with salsa and cheese prior to popping in the oven.

Cooked chicken or 1 1/2 cups (375 mL) small cooked shrimp can be used instead of turkey.

Amazing Turkey Enchiladas

PREHEAT OVEN TO 350° F (180° C)
13- BY 9-INCH (3 L) BAKING DISH, OILED

1/2 cup	light cream cheese	125 mL
1/2 cup	plain low-fat yogurt *or* light sour cream	125 mL
2 cups	cooked turkey, cut into thin strips	500 mL
3	green onions, finely chopped	3
2	tomatoes, seeded and diced	2
1/4 cup	chopped fresh coriander *or* parsley	50 mL
6	flour tortillas (8-inch [20 cm] size)	6
1 1/2 cups	mild or medium salsa	375 mL
1 cup	shredded Cheddar or Monterey Jack cheese	250 mL

1. Place cream cheese in a large bowl; microwave at Medium for 1 minute to soften. Stir well. Stir in yogurt, turkey, green onions, tomatoes and coriander.

2. Spread about 1/2 cup (125 mL) of the turkey mixture down center of each tortilla and roll up. Arrange tortillas in single layer, seam-side down, in baking dish. Spread with salsa and sprinkle with cheese. Bake for 30 to 35 minutes or until heated through. Sprinkle with extra chopped coriander, if desired.

TO MICROWAVE

Do not sprinkle with the cheese. Cover dish with waxed paper; microwave at Medium-High for 7 to 9 minutes or until heated through. Sprinkle with cheese; microwave at High for 1 minute or until cheese melts.

Per serving	
Calories	400
Protein	27 g
Carbohydrates	36 g
Dietary Fiber	4 g
Fat - Total	16 g
Saturated Fat	7.9 g
Calcium	263 mg

Quick Turkey Curry

This recipe will make you want to roast a turkey just so you have some leftovers on hand. But, if time does not permit, buy a roasted chicken from the deli section of the supermarket and use the diced meat in this no-fuss dish.

TIP

Mango chutney is called for in this recipe, but any type, whether store-bought or home-made can be used; add according to taste.

Serve over basmati rice and sprinkle with chopped coriander, if desired.

2 tsp	vegetable oil	10 mL
1	small onion, chopped	1
1	large clove garlic, minced	1
2 tsp	minced ginger root	10 mL
1	apple, peeled and chopped	1
1/2 cup	finely diced celery	125 mL
2 tsp	curry powder	10 mL
1 tbsp	all-purpose flour	15 mL
1 1/3 cups	chicken stock	325 mL
3 tbsp	mango chutney	45 mL
2 cups	diced cooked turkey or chicken	500 mL
1/4 cup	raisins	50 mL
	Salt and pepper	

1. In a large nonstick skillet, heat oil over medium heat. Add onions, garlic, ginger, apple, celery and curry powder; cook, stirring, for 5 minutes or until softened.
2. Blend in flour; add chicken stock and chutney. Cook, stirring, until sauce comes to a boil and thickens. Stir in turkey and raisins; season with salt and pepper to taste. Cook for 3 minutes or until heated through.

Per serving	
Calories	250
Protein	24 g
Carbohydrates	25 g
Dietary Fiber	2 g
Fat - Total	7 g
Saturated Fat	1.5 g
Calcium	50 mg

SERVES 4

Rosemary Beef Ragout

Stews are not generally considered fast cooking. However, they are very convenient for reheating and freezing, so they can be a real time saver. Keep stew in a covered container in the refrigerator for up to 3 days. Or, double the recipe and freeze half for another meal.

TIP

Substitute 1 large fennel bulb for the celery, if desired. Trim top from fennel; cut in half lengthwise and remove core. Cut into strips.

4 tsp	olive oil	20 mL
1 lb	stewing beef, cut into 1-inch (2.5 cm) cubes	500 g
1	large onion, chopped	2
3	cloves garlic, finely chopped	2
1 1/2 tsp	dried rosemary, crumbled	7 mL
2 tbsp	balsamic or red wine vinegar	25 mL
2 tbsp	all-purpose flour	25 mL
2 1/2 cups	beef stock	625 mL
2 tbsp	tomato paste	25 mL
1/2 tsp	salt	2 mL
1/2 tsp	pepper	2 mL
12 oz	baby carrots, peeled	375 g
1 1/2 cups	thickly sliced celery	375 mL

1. In a large Dutch oven or saucepan, heat half the oil over high heat. Brown beef in batches; transfer to a plate.

2. Add remaining oil to pan. Reduce heat to medium and add onion, garlic and rosemary; cook, stirring, for 3 minutes, or until softened. Add vinegar; cook until almost evaporated. Sprinkle with flour. Add stock, tomato paste, salt and pepper. Bring to a boil; cook, stirring, until slightly thickened.

3. Return meat and accumulated juices to pan; reduce heat, cover and simmer for 1 1/4 hours. Add carrots and celery; simmer, covered, for 30 minutes or until beef and vegetables are tender.

Per serving	
Calories	298
Protein	26 g
Carbohydrates	19 g
Dietary Fiber	2 g
Fat - Total	13 g
Saturated Fat	3.8 g
Calcium	78 mg

Veal Braised with Onions

Richly flavored braised meats like veal are always a welcome choice for a family meal. I make them in advance, since their flavor improves when refrigerated and reheated the next day. Serve this simple dish with noodles or creamy mashed potatoes.

TIP

To brown meat without having to add a lot of oil, pat meat dry with paper towels before cooking. Add a bit of the oil to the pan and heat until hot but not smoking. Add a small amount of the meat at a time until nicely colored; remove. Add a bit more oil to pan if necessary and reheat before adding next batch of meat.

2 lbs	lean stewing veal, cut into 3/4-inch (2 cm) cubes	1 kg
2 tbsp	olive oil	25 mL
2	large onions, chopped	2
2 tbsp	all-purpose flour	25 mL
1 1/2 cups	chicken stock	375 mL
1/2 cup	dry white wine *or* additional stock	125 mL
2 tbsp	tomato paste	25 mL
3/4 tsp	salt	4 mL
1/2 tsp	pepper	2 mL
1/4 cup	chopped parsley	50 mL
2	cloves garlic, minced	2
1 tsp	grated lemon zest	5 mL

1. In a large Dutch oven, heat half the oil over high heat; brown veal in batches. Transfer to a plate. Reduce heat to medium; add remaining oil. Add onions and cook, stirring, for 5 minutes or until lightly colored. Blend in flour; stir in stock, wine and tomato paste. Add veal along with accumulated juices; season with salt and pepper. Bring to a boil.

2. Reduce heat, cover and simmer, stirring occasionally, for 50 minutes. Stir in parsley, garlic and lemon zest; cook, covered, for 10 minutes or until veal is tender.

Per serving	
Calories	264
Protein	33 g
Carbohydrates	9 g
Dietary Fiber	1 g
Fat - Total	9 g
Saturated Fat	1.9 g
Calcium	48 mg

Make-Ahead Southwestern Pork Stew

Here's a soothing dish to serve for casual get-togethers. This stew requires no more preparation time than a stir-fry or one-pot dish. Cutting the meat into smaller pieces also shortens the cooking time.

TIP

Lean stewing beef can be substituted for the pork. For a vegetarian dish, replace meat with cubes of firm tofu. Add along with kidney beans.

1 lb	lean stewing pork, cut into 3/4-inch (2 cm) cubes	500 g
4 tsp	olive oil	20 mL
2	medium onions, chopped	2
3	cloves garlic, finely chopped	3
4 tsp	chili powder	20 mL
1 1/2 tsp	dried oregano	7 mL
1 tsp	ground cumin	5 mL
3/4 tsp	salt	4 mL
1/2 tsp	red pepper flakes	2 mL
3 tbsp	all-purpose flour	45 mL
2 cups	beef stock *or* chicken stock	500 mL
1	can (28 oz [796 mL]) tomatoes, chopped	1
2	bell peppers (assorted colors), cubed	2
2 cups	frozen corn kernels	500 mL
1	can (19 oz [540 mL]) kidney beans *or* black beans, rinsed and drained	1
	Chopped coriander (optional)	

1. In a large Dutch oven, heat half the oil over high heat; brown pork in batches. Transfer to a plate. Add remaining oil to pan; reduce heat to medium. Add onions, garlic, chili powder, oregano, cumin, salt and red pepper flakes; cook, stirring, for 2 minutes or until softened.

2. Sprinkle with flour; stir in stock and tomatoes. Bring to a boil, stirring until thickened. Return pork and accumulated juices to pan; reduce heat, cover and simmer for 1 hour or until meat is tender.

3. Add bell peppers, corn and kidney beans; simmer, covered, for 15 minutes or until vegetables are tender. Garnish with chopped coriander, if desired.

Per serving	
Calories	355
Protein	27 g
Carbohydrates	42 g
Dietary Fiber	10 g
Fat - Total	11 g
Saturated Fat	2.6 g
Calcium	101 mg

SERVES 4

Flash-in-the-Pan Pork with Couscous

Have your vegetables chopped and spices measured before you start the actual cooking. With all the ingredients ready to go in the skillet, this dish cooks in a flash.

TIP

Boneless chicken breasts are an ideal substitute for the pork. Use whatever vegetables you have on hand to replace carrots, broccoli and red pepper.

4 tsp	olive oil	20 mL
12 oz	lean pork loin or tenderloin, cut into thin strips	375 g
2	cloves garlic, minced	2
2 tsp	minced ginger root	10 mL
1 tsp	ground cumin	5 mL
1	red bell pepper, diced	1
2	small carrots, peeled and thinly sliced on the diagonal	2
2 cups	small broccoli florets	500 mL
3	green onions, chopped	3
1/4 cup	raisins	50 mL
1 1/4 cups	chicken stock *or* vegetable stock	300 mL
1/4 tsp	salt	1 mL
1/4 tsp	pepper	1 mL
1 cup	couscous	250 mL

1. In a large nonstick skillet, heat oil over medium-high heat. Add pork and cook, stirring, until no longer pink. Transfer to a plate. Add remaining oil to skillet; reduce heat to medium. Add garlic, ginger and cumin; cook, stirring, for 1 minute. Stir in red pepper, carrots, broccoli and 1/4 cup (50 mL) water. Cover and steam vegetables 2 to 3 minutes or until almost tender.

2. Return pork and any juices to skillet along with green onions, raisins, stock, salt and pepper. Bring to a boil. Stir in couscous; cover and remove from heat. Let stand for 7 minutes. Uncover and fluff with fork; let stand 2 more minutes before serving.

Per serving	
Calories	400
Protein	30 g
Carbohydrates	52 g
Dietary Fiber	5 g
Fat - Total	8 g
Saturated Fat	1.7 g
Calcium	66 mg

One-Pot Italian Sausages Braised with Potatoes

SERVES 4

This rustic dish is perfect with a glass of red wine on a wind-down Friday night. Do give the fennel a try; when raw, this up-and-coming vegetable has an assertive anise taste. However, when cooked, it's much more mellow and inviting.

TIP

Instead of fennel, use about 3 cups (750 mL) shredded cabbage.

1 lb	mild or hot Italian sausages	500 g
1 tbsp	olive oil	15 mL
1	large onion, halved lengthwise, sliced	1
1	large bulb fennel, trimmed, cored and cut into strips	1
2	cloves garlic, finely chopped	2
1 tsp	dried oregano	5 mL
4	medium potatoes, peeled and cubed	4
1	can (14 oz [398 mL]) tomatoes, chopped	1
1/2 cup	beef stock	125 mL
1/2 tsp	salt	2 mL
1/4 tsp	pepper	1 mL
2 tbsp	chopped parsley	25 mL

1. With a fork, prick sausages all over and place in large saucepan over medium-high heat. Add 2 tbsp (25 mL) water and cook, turning often and adding more water as needed (to prevent sausages from sticking), for 12 minutes or until browned and no longer pink in center. Transfer to a cutting board. Let cool slightly; cut into slices.

2. Drain any fat in pan; add oil, onion, fennel, garlic and oregano; cook, stirring, for 3 minutes or until softened. Add potatoes, tomatoes, stock, salt and pepper; bring to a boil. Reduce heat, cover and cook for 15 minutes or until potatoes are almost tender. Return sausage to pan; cover and cook for 8 minutes or until potatoes are tender. Sprinkle with parsley.

Per serving	
Calories	392
Protein	17 g
Carbohydrates	41 g
Dietary Fiber	6 g
Fat - Total	19 g
Saturated Fat	5.8 g
Calcium	106 mg

SERVES 4

This tasty sauce flecked with apples and dried cranberries also goes well with bonelesss chicken breasts or turkey scallops. Pair this dish with scalloped potatoes or rice and a green vegetable such as broccoli.

TIP

Pat ham dry with paper towels prior to browning.

Ham Steak with Apples and Cranberries

2/3 cup	apple cider or juice	150 mL
1 tbsp	packed brown sugar	15 mL
2 tsp	freshly squeezed lemon juice	10 mL
1 1/2 tsp	Dijon mustard	7 mL
1 1/2 tsp	cornstarch	7 mL
1 tbsp	butter	15 mL
1 lb	ham steak, trimmed and cut into 4 portions	500 g
2	green onions, chopped	2
1	apple, peeled, cored and diced	1
1/4 cup	dried cranberries *or* raisins	50 mL

1. In a glass measure, combine apple cider, brown sugar, lemon juice, mustard and cornstarch until smooth.

2. In a large nonstick skillet, heat butter over medium-high heat; brown ham on both sides. Remove to a plate.

3. Reduce heat to medium. Add green onions, apple and cranberries to skillet; cook, stirring, for 2 minutes or until softened. Add cider mixture; cook, stirring, until sauce thickens. Return ham to skillet; cook for 1 to 2 minutes or until heated through.

Per serving	
Calories	246
Protein	22 g
Carbohydrates	20 g
Dietary Fiber	2 g
Fat - Total	8 g
Saturated Fat	3.5 g
Calcium	59 mg

SERVES 4

Here's a simple meal-in-one dish to serve with a salad or steamed vegetables. When the ham is omitted, the recipe also does double-duty as a side or vegetarian dish.

TIP

Use your food processor to slice the potatoes quickly. When preparing ahead, layer potatoes in cream sauce in dish, cover and refrigerate for up to 4 hours.

Scalloped Potatoes with Ham and Swiss Cheese

PREHEAT OVEN TO 350° F (180° C)
11- BY 9-INCH (2.5 L) BAKING DISH, BUTTERED

2 tbsp	butter	25 mL
1	large onion, halved lengthwise, thinly sliced	1
2 tbsp	all-purpose flour	25 mL
1 1/2 cups	milk	375 mL
2 tsp	Dijon mustard	10 mL
1/2 tsp	salt	2 mL
	Nutmeg	
6	medium potatoes	6
8 oz	smoked ham, cut into 1-inch (2.5 cm) thin strips	250 g
1 cup	shredded Swiss or Cheddar cheese	250 mL

1. In a medium saucepan, melt butter over medium heat. Add onion and cook for 3 minutes or until softened. Sprinkle with flour; slowly stir in 1/2 cup (125 mL) of the milk; cook, stirring, until thickened. Stir in remaining milk, mustard, salt and nutmeg to taste. Bring to a boil; cook, stirring, until sauce thickens.

2. Peel and thinly slice potatoes. Rinse under cold water; drain. Wrap in a clean kitchen towel to dry. Stir into sauce; bring to a boil. Stir in ham strips. Pour into baking dish.

3. Sprinkle with cheese; bake for 45 minutes or until potatoes are tender and top is golden.

Per serving	
Calories	465
Protein	29 g
Carbohydrates	45 g
Dietary Fiber	3 g
Fat - Total	19 g
Saturated Fat	10.8 g
Calcium	412 mg

No trip to the fish market is required to make this quick main-course dish. Packaged frozen fish fillets work just fine. And here's an extra bonus — even with a small amount of light cream added, this dish is low in fat.

TIP

To defrost package of frozen fish fillets: Remove package wrapping; place fish on plate. Microwave at Medium for 3 minutes. Shield ends with thin strips of foil to prevent them from cooking before the rest of the fish has defrosted. Microwave at Defrost for 3 minutes more or until fish separates into fillets. Let stand for 10 minutes to complete defrosting. Pat dry with paper towels to absorb excess moisture.

Per serving	
Calories	146
Protein	17 g
Carbohydrates	6 g
Dietary Fiber	1 g
Fat - Total	5 g
Saturated Fat	2.6 g
Calcium	31 mg

Cod with Mushrooms and Tomato

PREHEAT OVEN TO 375° F (190° C)
8-INCH (2 L) SQUARE BAKING DISH

1	pkg (14 oz [400 g]) frozen cod, sole, turbot or haddock fillets, defrosted	1
	Salt and pepper	
1 1/2 cups	sliced mushrooms	375 mL
1	large tomato, seeded and diced	1
2	green onions, finely chopped	2
2 tbsp	chopped fresh dill *or* parsley	25 mL
1/3 cup	dry white wine *or* fish stock	75 mL
1 tbsp	cornstarch	15 mL
1/3 cup	light (10 %) cream	75 mL

1. Arrange fish fillets in a single layer in baking dish; season with salt and pepper. Layer with mushrooms, tomato, green onions and dill. Pour wine or stock over. Bake for 20 to 25 minutes or until fish is opaque and flakes when tested with fork.

2. Remove from oven; carefully pour juices from dish into small saucepan. (Place a large plate or lid over dish). Return fish to turned-off oven to keep warm.

3. In a glass measuring cup, blend cornstarch with 2 tbsp (25 mL) cold water; stir in cream. Add to saucepan. Place over medium heat; cook, whisking, until sauce comes to a boil and thickens. Season with salt and pepper to taste. (Sauce will be thick.) Pour over fish and serve.

SERVES 4

Skillet Shrimp and Rice Creole

Attractive and colorful, this classic Southern specialty relies on the flavors of tomato, celery, thyme and bay leaf. It's a spicy one-dish meal that takes only 30 minutes to cook.

TIP

Today supermarkets stock frozen shrimp already peeled and deveined — a convenient option for this recipe.

VARIATION

Skillet Sausage and Rice Creole
Substitute 12 oz (375 g) mild or hot Italian sausages for the shrimp. Cut sausages in half lengthwise. Place cut-side down in skillet; cook over medium heat, turning occasionally, for 10 minutes or until no longer pink. Cut into thick slices; add to recipe as you would the shrimp.

1 tbsp	vegetable oil	15 mL
1	large onion, chopped	1
2	cloves garlic, finely chopped	2
2	stalks celery, chopped	2
1/2 tsp	dried thyme	2 mL
1	bay leaf	1
1 cup	long-grain white rice	250 mL
1	red bell pepper, diced	1
1	can (14 oz [398 mL]) tomatoes, chopped	1
1 cup	fish stock *or* chicken stock	250 mL
1/2 tsp	salt	2 mL
Pinch	cayenne pepper	Pinch
2	small zucchini, halved lengthwise and thinly sliced	2
1 lb	large shrimp, peeled and deveined, tails left on	500 g

1. In a large nonstick skillet, heat oil over medium heat. Add onion, garlic, celery, thyme and bay leaf; cook, stirring, for 5 minutes or until softened.

2. Stir in rice and red pepper; cook for 2 minutes. Add tomatoes, stock, salt and a generous pinch cayenne pepper. Bring to a boil; reduce heat, cover and simmer for 15 minutes. Stir in zucchini; bury shrimp in rice. Cover and cook for 8 minutes or until zucchini are tender and shrimp are pink and firm.

Per serving	
Calories	362
Protein	25 g
Carbohydrates	53 g
Dietary Fiber	4 g
Fat - Total	5 g
Saturated Fat	0.7 g
Calcium	130 mg

Easy Curried Fish Stew

Ginger root adds a sparking flavor to this low-cal stew. Serve steaming bowls with chunks of crusty whole grain bread. It's a complete meal!

TIP

Instead of fish, add 1 1/2 cups (375 mL) of small cooked shrimp.

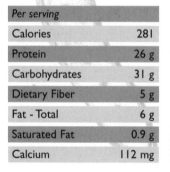

1 tbsp	vegetable oil	15 mL
1	small onion, finely chopped	1
1 tbsp	minced ginger root	15 mL
2 tsp	curry powder	10 mL
2 cups	diced peeled potatoes	500 mL
1 1/2 cups	thinly sliced carrots	375 mL
2 1/4 cups	fish stock *or* chicken stock	550 mL
1 tbsp	cornstarch	15 mL
	Salt and pepper	
1 1/2 cups	snow peas, ends trimmed, halved	375 mL
1 lb	fish fillets, cut into chunks	500 g

1. In large saucepan, heat oil over medium heat. Add onions, ginger and curry powder; cook, stirring, for 2 minutes or until softened. Add potatoes, carrots and fish stock. Bring to a boil; reduce heat, cover and simmer for 10 to 12 minutes or until vegetables are just tender.

2. In a bowl, blend cornstarch with 2 tbsp (25 mL) water. Add to stew and cook, stirring, until thickened. Season with salt and pepper to taste. Stir in snow peas and fish; cover and cook for 2 to 3 minutes or until snow peas are tender-crisp and fish is opaque.

Per serving	
Calories	281
Protein	26 g
Carbohydrates	31 g
Dietary Fiber	5 g
Fat - Total	6 g
Saturated Fat	0.9 g
Calcium	112 mg

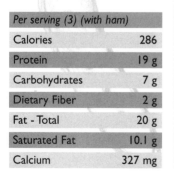

SERVES 2 TO 3

Versatile mushrooms star in this terrific dish that's perfect to serve for brunch or a light supper.

TIP

Use a variety of white and exotic mushrooms such as shiitake, portobello and oyster. Herbed soft goat cheese can replace the cream cheese, if desired.

Cheese and Mushroom Oven Omelette

PREHEAT OVEN TO 350° F (180° C)
WELL-BUTTERED 9- OR 10- INCH (23 OR 25 CM) PIE PLATE
SPRINKLED WITH 1 TBSP (15 mL) FINE DRY BREAD CRUMBS

4	large eggs, separated	4
2 tbsp	milk	25 mL
	Salt and pepper	
1 tbsp	butter	15 mL
3 cups	sliced assorted mushrooms	750 mL
3	green onions, chopped	3
1/4 cup	light or herb cream cheese	50 mL
1/3 cup	shredded Cheddar cheese	75 mL
2 oz	smoked ham, cut into thin strips *or* 3 slices bacon, cooked crisp and crumbled	60 g

1. In a small bowl, beat egg yolks with milk; season with salt and pepper. In a bowl using an electric mixer, beat egg whites until stiff peaks form. Slowly beat in yolk mixture on low speed until blended into egg whites. Pour into pie plate. Bake for 15 minutes or until just set in the center.

2. Meanwhile, in a large nonstick skillet, melt butter over medium-high heat. Cook mushrooms and green onions, stirring, for 5 minutes or until tender and liquid is evaporated. Remove from heat; stir in cream cheese until smooth.

3. Spoon evenly over omelette; sprinkle with cheese and ham. Bake for 8 minutes more or until cheese is melted.

Per serving (3) (with ham)	
Calories	286
Protein	19 g
Carbohydrates	7 g
Dietary Fiber	2 g
Fat - Total	20 g
Saturated Fat	10.1 g
Calcium	327 mg

SERVES 6

You can always count on eggs for an economical meal. This oven-baked crustless quiche is perfect for brunch or an easy supper, served with juicy sliced tomatoes and good bread.

TIP

Wrap zucchini in a clean dry kitchen towel to remove excess moisture.

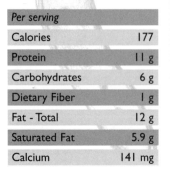

Crustless Zucchini Quiche

PREHEAT OVEN TO 325° F (160° C)
10-INCH (25 CM) PIE PLATE OR QUICHE DISH, BUTTERED

1 tbsp	butter	15 mL
3 cups	grated zucchini (unpeeled), squeezed dry	750 mL
4	green onions, chopped	4
1	red bell pepper, diced	1
6	eggs	6
3/4 cup	shredded Cheddar or Fontina cheese	175 mL
1/2 cup	soft bread crumbs	125 mL
1/4 tsp	salt	1 mL
1/4 tsp	pepper	1 mL

1. In a large nonstick skillet, melt butter over medium-high heat. Add zucchini, green onions and red pepper; cook, stirring often, for 5 minutes or until softened. Let cool slightly.

2. In a large bowl, beat eggs; stir in zucchini mixture, cheese, bread crumbs, salt and pepper. Pour into pie plate. Bake for 35 to 40 minutes or until set in center.

Per serving	
Calories	177
Protein	11 g
Carbohydrates	6 g
Dietary Fiber	1 g
Fat - Total	12 g
Saturated Fat	5.9 g
Calcium	141 mg

Main Courses

Stuffed Mediterranean Chicken for Company

SERVES 4

Here's what I serve when I'm entertaining and I want a dish that can be prepared ahead to pop in the oven as guests come through the door. Keep the rest of the menu just as uncomplicated by serving fettuccine or your favorite pasta and a green vegetable.

TIP

To prepare this dish ahead: Arrange browned chicken breasts in shallow baking dish; pour prepared sauce over. Let cool, cover and refrigerate up to 1 day ahead. Bake, covered, in a 350° F (180° C) oven for about 35 minutes or until chicken is no longer pink inside.

If using dry-packed sun-dried tomatoes, cover with boiling water and let soak for 10 minutes or until softened.

To toast pine nuts, place in a dry skillet over medium heat, stirring, for 2 to 3 minutes or until lightly colored. Watch carefully, as they burn easily.

1/4 cup	chopped sun-dried tomatoes	50 mL
1/4 cup	chopped parsley	50 mL
2 tbsp	lightly toasted pine nuts	25 mL
2 tbsp	grated Parmesan cheese	25 mL
4	large skinless, boneless chicken breasts	4
	Salt and pepper	
2 tbsp	all-purpose flour	25 mL
1 tbsp	olive oil	15 mL
1/2 cup	chicken stock	125 mL
1/3 cup	dry white wine	75 mL
2	cloves garlic, minced	2
3	tomatoes, peeled, seeded and diced	3
1/4 cup	slivered pitted Kalamata olives	50 mL
1 tbsp	capers (optional)	15 mL

1. In a bowl combine sun-dried tomatoes, half the parsley, pine nuts and Parmesan cheese. With a sharp knife, slice each chicken breast lengthwise along one side, almost in half. Open each breast like a book; season with salt and pepper. Spoon in parsley mixture; fold top over and press gently to seal.

2. On a plate, lightly dredge breasts in flour, shaking off excess. In a large nonstick skillet, heat oil over medium-high heat. Add chicken and cook until lightly browned on both sides. Remove to a plate.

3. Reduce heat to medium. Stir in stock, wine and garlic; cook for 1 minute. Stir in tomatoes, olives, capers (if using), and remaining parsley; cook 2 to 3 minutes or until slightly reduced and thickened. Season with salt and pepper to taste; return chicken to skillet. Return to a boil; reduce heat, cover and simmer 10 to 15 minutes or until chicken is no longer pink inside. Cut chicken into diagonal slices. Spoon sauce onto plates; arrange chicken on top.

Per serving	
Calories	310
Protein	32 g
Carbohydrates	14 g
Dietary Fiber	2 g
Fat - Total	13 g
Saturated Fat	2.7 g
Calcium	85 mg

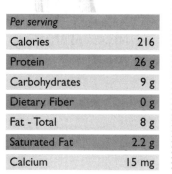

SERVES 4

Kids love simple dishes like this one, with its straightforward flavors. And this chicken dish is simple enough that even young cooks can make it.

TIP

This recipe also works well with a whole cut-up chicken or bone-in chicken breasts. With its tang of lemon and sweetness of honey, this dish is sure to become a family favorite.

Just-For-Kids Honey Lemon Chicken

PREHEAT OVEN TO 350° F (180° C)
13- BY 9-INCH (3 L) BAKING DISH

4	chicken legs, skinned	4
2 tbsp	honey	25 mL
2 tsp	grated lemon zest	10 mL
1 tsp	freshly squeezed lemon juice	5 mL
1	large clove garlic, minced	1
1/4 tsp	salt	1 mL
1/4 tsp	pepper	1 mL

1. Arrange chicken in baking dish. In a bowl combine honey, lemon zest, lemon juice, garlic, salt and pepper; spoon over chicken.
2. Bake in oven, basting once, for 45 to 55 minutes or until juices run clear when chicken is pierced.

Per serving	
Calories	216
Protein	26 g
Carbohydrates	9 g
Dietary Fiber	0 g
Fat - Total	8 g
Saturated Fat	2.2 g
Calcium	15 mg

Who has time to wait around for a chicken to roast when you're in a hurry? I take an hour off the roasting time by doing two things: I cut the bird open along the backbone, place it flat on the broiler pan and then boost the oven temperature. The result? A golden, succulent bird in half the time.

TIP

Tucking herbs and garlic under the skin keeps the chicken juicy and flavorful. This treatment works well with chicken breasts, too.

One-Hour Roast Chicken with Sage and Garlic

PREHEAT OVEN TO 375° F (190° C)
BROILER PAN, OILED

1	chicken (3 1/2 lbs [1.75 kg])	1
1 tbsp	butter, softened	15 mL
2	cloves garlic, minced	2
1 tbsp	minced fresh sage (or 1 tsp [5 mL] crumbled dried sage)	15 mL
1 1/2 tsp	grated lemon zest	7 mL
1/2 tsp	salt	2 mL
1/2 tsp	pepper	2 mL
2 tsp	olive oil	10 mL
1/4 tsp	paprika	1 mL

1. Rinse and pat chicken dry inside and out with paper towels. Using heavy-duty kitchen scissors, cut chicken open along backbone; flatten and arrange skin-side up on rack of a broiler pan.

2. In a bowl, blend butter with garlic, sage, lemon zest, salt and pepper. Gently lift breast skin; using a knife or spatula, spread butter mixture under skin to coat breasts and part of legs. Press down on outside skin to smooth and spread butter mixture.

3. In a small bowl, combine olive oil and paprika; brush over chicken.

4. Roast chicken for 1 hour or until juices run clear and a meat thermometer inserted in the thickest part of the thigh registers 175° F (75° C). Transfer chicken to a platter. Tent with foil; let rest 5 minutes before carving.

Per serving (without skin)	
Calories	296
Protein	42 g
Carbohydrates	1 g
Dietary Fiber	0 g
Fat - Total	13 g
Saturated Fat	3.9 g
Calcium	28 mg

My Favorite Chicken Dish

Boneless chicken breasts are a staple in my weekly grocery cart. Everyone needs an all-purpose chicken dish to whip up on the spur of the moment. This is one of mine. It's a breeze to cook and always a hit with my family.

TIP

Vary the flavors by using different herbs such as tarragon or *herbes de Provence*. Serve this dish alongside noodles or rice. Add a salad and you've got dinner ready in 30 minutes.

4	skinless boneless chicken breasts	4
2 tbsp	all-purpose flour	25 mL
1/2 tsp	salt	2 mL
1/2 tsp	pepper	2 mL
1 tbsp	butter	15 mL
1/2 cup	chicken stock	125 mL
1/2 cup	orange juice (*or* mixture of juice and part dry white wine)	125 mL
1	large clove garlic, finely chopped	1
1/2 tsp	dried Italian herbs *or* basil	2 mL
1/4 tsp	granulated sugar	1 mL
1 tbsp	chopped parsley *or* chives	15 mL

1. On a cutting board using a sharp knife, cut each breast lengthwise into 2 thin pieces. Place flour in a shallow bowl; season with salt and pepper. Coat chicken in flour mixture, shaking off excess.

2. Heat a large nonstick skillet over medium-high heat. Add butter; when foamy, add chicken pieces. Cook 2 minutes per side or until lightly browned. Transfer to a plate.

3. Reduce heat to medium; add stock, orange juice, garlic, Italian herbs and sugar to skillet. Bring to a boil; cook for 1 minute or until slightly reduced. Season sauce with salt and pepper to taste. Return chicken to skillet; reduce heat, cover and simmer for 5 minutes or until no longer pink inside and sauce is slightly thickened. Serve sprinkled with parsley.

Per serving	
Calories	204
Protein	28 g
Carbohydrates	7 g
Dietary Fiber	0 g
Fat - Total	6 g
Saturated Fat	2.7 g
Calcium	23 mg

Known as *shish taouk*, these kabobs are fast food in the Middle East. I find the Mediterranean blend of lemon, olive oil and garlic used here very appealing with chicken. You can also use the versatile marinade for chicken breasts and legs.

TIP

Turn kabobs into sandwich wraps by nestling the grilled chicken in warm pita breads along with shredded lettuce, tomato wedges and chopped onion. Top with a spoonful of store-bought hummus, mayonnaise flavored with garlic or tzatziki sauce. Roll up for a quick meal.

Lebanese Chicken Kabobs

PREHEAT BARBECUE GRILL OR BROILER

1/4 cup	plain low-fat yogurt	50 mL
2 tbsp	olive oil	25 mL
2 tbsp	freshly squeezed lemon juice	25 mL
2 tbsp	chopped fresh mint (or 1 tsp [5 mL] dried)	25 mL
2	cloves garlic, minced	2
1/2 tsp	salt	2 mL
1/4 tsp	pepper	1 mL
4	skinless boneless chicken breasts, cut into 1-inch (2.5 cm) cubes	4

1. In a medium bowl, combine yogurt, olive oil, lemon juice, mint, garlic, salt and pepper. Add chicken to marinade; cover and refrigerate for 1 hour or overnight.

2. Remove from refrigerator 30 minutes before cooking. If using wooden skewers, soak in cold water for 30 minutes.

3. Thread chicken onto skewers. Place on greased grill or preheated stovetop grill pan over medium-high heat; cook, turning occasionally, for about 12 minutes or until chicken is no longer pink inside. Or, arrange kabobs on broiler rack. Place under preheated broiler 4 inches (10 cm) from heat; cook, turning occasionally, for about 15 minutes or until chicken is no longer pink inside.

Per serving	
Calories	170
Protein	27 g
Carbohydrates	1 g
Dietary Fiber	0 g
Fat - Total	5 g
Saturated Fat	1.3 g
Calcium	32 mg

INDIAN-STYLE GRILLED CHICKEN BREASTS (PAGE 97)
OVERLEAF: SPANISH VEGETABLE PAELLA (PAGE 131)

Indian-Style Grilled Chicken Breasts

Ginger, cumin, coriander and cayenne pepper are signature ingredients in Indian cooking. Not only do they make chicken taste wonderful, but I love the way the spicy yogurt marinade keeps it moist and tender.

TIP

If you have time, let the chicken marinate for several hours or overnight in the refrigerator to intensify the flavors. To avoid bacterial contamination, baste the chicken only once halfway through cooking, then discard any leftover marinade.

PREHEAT BARBECUE GRILL OR OVEN TO 350° F (180° C)
BAKING SHEET WITH RACK

1/2 cup	plain low-fat yogurt	125 mL
1 tbsp	tomato paste	15 mL
2	green onions, coarsely chopped	2
2	cloves garlic, quartered	2
1	piece (1-inch [2.5 cm]) peeled ginger root, coarsely chopped (or 1 tsp [5 mL] ground ginger)	1
1/2 tsp	ground cumin	2 mL
1/2 tsp	ground coriander	2 mL
1/2 tsp	salt	2 mL
1/4 tsp	cayenne pepper	1 mL
4	chicken breasts (bone-in)	4
2 tbsp	chopped fresh coriander *or* parsley	25 mL

1. In a food processor, combine yogurt, tomato paste, green onions, garlic, ginger, cumin, coriander, salt and cayenne pepper; purée until smooth.

2. Arrange chicken in a shallow dish; coat with yogurt mixture. Cover and refrigerate for 1 hour or up to 1 day ahead. Remove from refrigerator 30 minutes before cooking.

3. Place chicken skin-side down on greased grill over medium-high heat; cook for 15 minutes. Brush with marinade; turn and cook for 10 to 15 minutes longer or until golden and juices run clear. (Or place chicken on rack set on baking sheet; roast, basting after 30 minutes with marinade, for 50 to 55 minutes or until juices run clear.) Serve garnished with chopped coriander.

Per serving (without skin)	
Calories	213
Protein	31 g
Carbohydrates	3 g
Dietary Fiber	1 g
Fat - Total	8 g
Saturated Fat	2.3 g
Calcium	55 mg

< QUICK BISTRO-STYLE STEAK (PAGE 105) WITH ROASTED GARLIC POTATOES (PAGE 150)

Honey-Dijon Turkey Schnitzel

Turkey is no longer just for holidays. In fact, the turkey cutlets now sold in supermarkets rival traditional veal cutlets in popularity — and they're more economical. The crumb-coating method used here is a tasty way to dress them up.

TIP

This recipe also works well with thin veal and pork cutlets or boneless chicken breasts cut into thin slices. For easy slicing, freeze chicken breasts for 20 to 30 minutes until firm.

2 tbsp	freshly squeezed lemon juice	25 mL
4 tsp	honey	20 mL
4 tsp	Dijon mustard	20 mL
1 lb	thin turkey cutlets	500 g
2/3 cup	dry seasoned bread crumbs	150 mL
1/4 cup	grated Parmesan cheese	50 mL
2 tbsp	vegetable oil (approximate)	25 mL

1. In a bowl combine lemon juice, honey and mustard. Add turkey cutlets; stir to coat well.

2. In a shallow bowl, combine bread crumbs and Parmesan cheese. Dip turkey in crumb mixture to coat evenly.

3. In a large nonstick skillet, heat 1 tbsp (15 mL) of the oil over medium heat. Cook turkey in batches, adding more oil as needed, for about 1 1/2 to 2 minutes for each side or until browned and no longer pink in center.

Per serving	
Calories	325
Protein	36 g
Carbohydrates	21 g
Dietary Fiber	1 g
Fat - Total	10 g
Saturated Fat	2.1 g
Calcium	126 mg

Orange-Basil Chicken Stir-Fry

In this family favorite, orange juice and balsamic vinegar combine to give the chicken and vegetables a delightful sweet-sour tang.

TIP

Lean boneless pork loin chops or tenderloin make a great substitute for the chicken. Serve over noodles or rice.

Instead of dried basil, substitute 2 tbsp (25 mL) chopped fresh basil; add at end of cooking.

1/3 cup	orange juice	75 mL
1/4 cup	chicken stock	50 mL
2 tbsp	balsamic vinegar	25 mL
1 tbsp	granulated sugar	15 mL
2 tsp	grated orange zest	10 mL
2 tsp	cornstarch	10 mL
1/4 tsp	salt	1 mL
4 tsp	vegetable oil	20 mL
1 lb	lean boneless chicken breasts, cut into strips	500 g
2	medium zucchini, halved lengthwise and sliced	2
1	red bell pepper, cut into thin 2-inch (5 cm) strips	1
1	large clove garlic, minced	1
1 tsp	dried basil	5 mL

1. In a glass measuring cup, combine orange juice, stock, vinegar, sugar, orange zest, cornstarch and salt; stir until smooth.

2. In a large nonstick skillet, heat half the oil over high heat. Add chicken and cook, stirring, for 3 minutes or until browned. Transfer to a plate.

3. Add remaining oil to skillet. Add zucchini, red pepper, garlic and basil; cook, stirring, for 2 minutes or until softened. Return pork to skillet; stir in stock mixture. Cook, stirring occasionally, for 2 minutes more or until sauce thickens and vegetables are tender-crisp.

Per serving	
Calories	217
Protein	24 g
Carbohydrates	13 g
Dietary Fiber	2 g
Fat - Total	8 g
Saturated Fat	1.1 g
Calcium	31 mg

SERVES 6

Balsamic-Glazed Chicken

The spicy-sweet baste keeps the chicken extra moist when grilled or oven-baked.

TIP

Oven method: Place chicken on greased foil-lined baking sheet; bake for 30 minutes. Brush with prepared marinade; bake for 15 to 20 minutes, basting often, until nicely glazed and juices run clear when chicken is pierced.

PREHEAT BARBECUE GRILL OR OVEN TO 375° F (190° C)

6	chicken legs	6
1/2 cup	orange juice	125 mL
1 tsp	grated orange zest	5 mL
1/4 cup	balsamic vinegar	50 mL
1 tbsp	olive oil	15 mL
2	cloves garlic, minced	2
1 1/2 tsp	dried basil	7 mL
1/2 tsp	salt	2 mL
1/2 tsp	red pepper flakes	2 mL
1/4 cup	Seville orange marmalade	50 mL

1. Remove skins from chicken; separate into drumsticks and thighs. In a large bowl, whisk together orange juice, orange zest, vinegar, oil, garlic, basil, salt and red pepper flakes; add chicken and toss to coat. Cover and refrigerate for 2 hours or overnight.

2. Reserving marinade, place chicken on greased grill over medium heat; close lid and cook, turning once, for 25 to 30 minutes or until golden brown. Meanwhile, in a saucepan, bring reserved marinade and marmalade to a boil; cook, stirring, for 3 minutes or until slightly thickened. Brush half over chicken; cook, turning often and brushing with remaining marinade, for 10 minutes or until juices run clear when chicken is pierced.

Per serving	
Calories	253
Protein	26 g
Carbohydrates	13 g
Dietary Fiber	0 g
Fat - Total	10 g
Saturated Fat	2.5 g
Calcium	29 mg

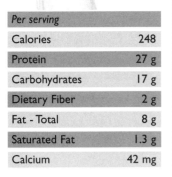

SERVES 4

Apples have always been paired with pork but pears deserve equal treatment. Here they make an especially delicious companion to this versatile meat.

TIP

Serve with rice and a steamed green vegetable such as snow peas, along with red pepper or broccoli.

Pork with Pears, Honey and Thyme

1 tbsp	vegetable oil	15 mL
1 lb	thin boneless pork loin chops (about 8)	500 g
2	pears, peeled, cored and thinly sliced	2
3	green onions, chopped	3
1 tbsp	honey	15 mL
1/2 tsp	dried thyme	2 mL
1/2 cup	chicken stock	125 mL
1 tbsp	cider vinegar	15 mL
1 tsp	cornstarch	5 mL
1/4 tsp	salt	1 mL
1/4 tsp	pepper	1 mL

1. In a large nonstick skillet, heat oil over medium-high heat; brown pork for 2 minutes on each side. Remove to a plate and keep warm. Add pears, green onions, honey and thyme to skillet; cook, stirring, for 2 to 3 minutes or until pears are softened.

2. Meanwhile, in a bowl, combine stock, vinegar, cornstarch, salt and pepper. Pour into skillet; cook, stirring, until slightly thickened. Return pork and any accumulated juices to skillet and cook, turning occasionally, for 1 to 2 minutes or until heated through.

Per serving	
Calories	248
Protein	27 g
Carbohydrates	17 g
Dietary Fiber	2 g
Fat - Total	8 g
Saturated Fat	1.3 g
Calcium	42 mg

SERVES 4

Everyone loves a big mess of ribs. Hide the knives and forks. Here comes a finger-licking good time!

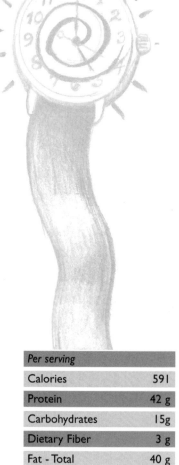

Tex-Mex Barbecue Spareribs

PREHEAT BARBECUE GRILL OR OVEN TO 375° F (190° C)

3 lbs	spareribs	1.5 kg
2 cups	TEX-MEX BARBECUE SAUCE (see recipe, facing page)	500 mL

1. Cut ribs into serving-sized pieces. Place in Dutch oven or large saucepan of boiling salted water; reduce heat, cover and simmer for 40 minutes or until tender. Drain.

2. Place ribs on greased grill over medium heat; cook, turning and basting often with sauce, for 15 to 20 minutes or until glazed and tender. Or, place ribs on foil-lined baking sheet. Generously brush both sides of ribs with sauce. Roast, uncovered, brushing often with sauce, for 25 to 30 minutes or until glazed and tender.

Per serving	
Calories	591
Protein	42 g
Carbohydrates	15g
Dietary Fiber	3 g
Fat - Total	40 g
Saturated Fat	14.5 g
Calcium	93 mg

Tex-Mex Barbecue Sauce

There are plenty of store-bought barbecue sauces, but none compares to the versatility and popularity of this lip-smackin' sauce. It has a spicy kick to it, but for those who crave it really hot, add more red pepper flakes or your favorite hot sauce.

Don't limit the sauce to just ribs; it's also terrific with other grill favorites such as burgers, pork chops and kabobs, or try it on chicken wings and legs. This makes a big batch; store extra sauce in a covered container in the refrigerator for up to 1 month. Or, freeze it.

1	bottle (12 oz [341 mL]) beer	1
2 cups	bottled chili sauce *or* ketchup	500 mL
1/2 cup	cider vinegar	125 mL
1/2 cup	packed brown sugar	125 mL
1/4 cup	Worcestershire sauce	50 mL
2	medium onions, finely chopped	2
4	large cloves garlic, minced	4
2 tbsp	chili powder	25 mL
1 tbsp	dried oregano	15 mL
1 tsp	red pepper flakes	5 mL

1. In a large saucepan, combine beer, chili sauce, cider vinegar, brown sugar, Worcestershire sauce, onions, garlic, chili powder, oregano and red pepper flakes. Bring to a boil; reduce heat and simmer, partially covered, stirring occasionally, for 25 minutes or until thickened.

Per 1/4 cup (50 mL)	
Calories	85
Protein	1 g
Carbohydrates	19 g
Dietary Fiber	1 g
Fat - Total	0 g
Saturated Fat	0 g
Calcium	30 mg

Here's a fast stir-fry that doesn't require a lot of chopping. Serve with steamed rice, cooked rice vermicelli or a string pasta such as linguine.

TIP

Substitute boneless chicken breast or pork tenderloin for the beef.

Easy Beef and Broccoli Stir-Fry

1 lb	lean boneless sirloin steak, cut into thin strips	500 g
2 tbsp	hoisin sauce	25 mL
2	cloves garlic, minced	2
1 tbsp	minced ginger root	15 mL
1 tsp	grated orange zest	5 mL
1/2 cup	orange juice	125 mL
3 tbsp	soya sauce	45 mL
2 tsp	cornstarch	10 mL
1/4 tsp	red pepper flakes	1 mL
1 tbsp	vegetable oil	15 mL
6 cups	small broccoli florets and peeled chopped stems (about 1 large bunch)	1.5 L
4	green onions, chopped	4

1. In a bowl toss beef strips with hoisin sauce, garlic and ginger. Let marinate at room temperature for 15 minutes. (Cover and refrigerate if preparing ahead.) In a glass measuring cup, combine orange zest and juice, soya sauce, cornstarch and red pepper flakes.

2. In a large nonstick skillet, heat oil over high heat; cook beef, stirring, for 2 minutes or until no longer pink. Remove to a plate.

3. Add broccoli and soya sauce mixture to skillet; reduce heat to medium, cover and cook for 2 to 3 minutes or until broccoli is tender-crisp. Add beef strips with any accumulated juices and green onions; cook, stirring, for 1 minute or until heated through.

Per serving	
Calories	290
Protein	31 g
Carbohydrates	17 g
Dietary Fiber	4 g
Fat - Total	11 g
Saturated Fat	3.4 g
Calcium	75 mg

Quick Bistro-Style Steak

Beef is back – and that includes the mighty steak, but in well-trimmed portions. Dressed up with wine, garlic and herbs, this steak recipe becomes a special dish when you're entertaining friends.

TIP

Serve with ROASTED GARLIC POTATOES (see recipe, page 150).

Herbes de Provence is a blend of French herbs that often includes thyme, rosemary, basil and sage. If you can't find this blend in your supermarket, substitute a generous pinch of each of these herbs.

4	boneless striploin steaks, each 6 oz (175 g])	4
1/2 tsp	coarsely ground black pepper	2 mL
2 tsp	olive oil	10 mL
2 tsp	butter	10 mL
	Salt	
1/4 cup	finely chopped shallots	50 mL
1	large clove garlic, finely chopped	1
1/4 tsp	*herbes de Provence*	1 mL
1/3 cup	red wine *or* additional stock	75 mL
1/2 cup	beef stock	125 mL
1 tbsp	Dijon mustard	15 mL
2 tbsp	chopped parsley	25 mL

1. Remove steaks from refrigerator 30 minutes before cooking. Season with pepper.
2. Heat a large heavy skillet over medium heat until hot; add oil and butter. Increase heat to high; brown steaks about 1 minute on each side. Reduce heat to medium; cook to desired degree of doneness. Transfer to a heated serving platter; season with salt and keep warm.
3. Add shallots, garlic and *herbes* to skillet; cook, stirring, for 1 minute. Stir in red wine; cook, scraping up any brown bits from bottom of pan, until liquid has almost evaporated.
4. Stir in stock, mustard and parsley; season with salt and pepper to taste. Cook, stirring, until slightly reduced. Spoon sauce over steaks. Serve immediately.

Per serving	
Calories	329
Protein	40 g
Carbohydrates	3 g
Dietary Fiber	0 g
Fat - Total	15 g
Saturated Fat	6.2 g
Calcium	33 mg

Here's my favorite way to prepare beef on the barbecue.
Flank steak is economical, easy
to marinate ahead, and leftovers
make great-tasting sandwiches.

TIP

Flank steak becomes more tender the longer it's marinated.
Thick-cut round steak can also
be prepared in the same way.

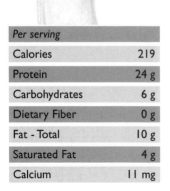

Per serving	
Calories	219
Protein	24 g
Carbohydrates	6 g
Dietary Fiber	0 g
Fat - Total	10 g
Saturated Fat	4 g
Calcium	11 mg

Easy Asian Flank Steak

PREHEAT BARBECUE GRILL OR BROILER

1/4 cup	hoisin sauce	50 mL
2 tbsp	soya sauce	25 mL
2 tbsp	freshly squeezed lime juice	25 mL
1 tbsp	vegetable oil	15 mL
4	cloves garlic, minced	4
2 tsp	Oriental chili paste (or 1 tsp [5 mL] red pepper flakes)	10 mL
1 1/2 lbs	flank steak	750 g

1. In a shallow glass dish, whisk together hoisin sauce, soya sauce, lime juice, oil, garlic and chili paste; add steak, turning to coat both sides with marinade. Refrigerate, covered, at least 8 hours or up to 24 hours. Remove meat from refrigerator 30 minutes before cooking.

2. Reserving the marinade, place steak on a greased grill over medium-high heat. Cook, basting often with mari- nade, for 7 to 8 minutes per side or until medium-rare. (Alternately, place steak on foil-lined baking sheet; broil 4 inches (10 cm) below preheated broiler for 7 to 8 min- utes on each side.) Transfer to cutting board, cover loosely with foil; let stand 10 minutes. Thinly slice at right angles to the grain of meat.

Lemon-Herb Veal Scalloppine

Here's a dish you could order in an Italian restaurant but you can make it just as easily at home — and in no time at all. There's little chopping required, so dinner is ready in less than 30 minutes.

TIP

Make your own Italian herb mixture by combining dried basil, oregano, rosemary and marjoram. Serve veal over noodles with steamed green beans or broccoli.

1/4 cup	all-purpose flour	50 mL
1/2 tsp	salt	2 mL
1/2 tsp	pepper	2 mL
1 lb	thin veal cutlets	500 g
4 tsp	olive oil (approximate)	20 mL
1/2 cup	chicken stock	125 mL
1/4 cup	dry white wine *or* additional stock	50 mL
1/2 tsp	dried Italian herbs	2 mL
1 tsp	grated lemon zest	5 mL
1 tbsp	freshly squeezed lemon juice	15 mL
2 tbsp	chopped parsley	25 mL

1. On a plate stir together the flour, salt and pepper. Coat veal in flour mixture, shaking off excess. In a large non-stick skillet, heat half the oil over high heat; cook veal in batches, adding more oil as needed, for 1 minute per side or until browned. Transfer to a plate and keep warm.

2. Reduce heat to medium. Add stock, wine and Italian herbs to skillet; cook, stirring, until slightly reduced. Stir in lemon zest, lemon juice, and parsley. Return veal to skillet; cook, turning occasionally, for 1 to 2 minutes or until heated through and sauce is slightly thickened. Season with salt and pepper to taste.

Per serving	
Calories	218
Protein	28 g
Carbohydrates	5 g
Dietary Fiber	0 g
Fat - Total	8 g
Saturated Fat	1.8 g
Calcium	14 mg

Lamb Chops with Maple-Mustard Baste

SERVES 4

Lamb chops are wonderful *au naturel*, but even more wonderful with a mustard glaze and a sweet hint of maple. Here's a quick and tasty way to dress up lamb chops when entertaining.

TIP

Try this marinade with lamb kabobs as well as chicken and pork.

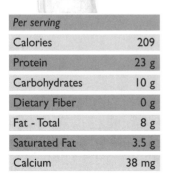

PREHEAT BARBECUE GRILL, STOVETOP GRILL OR BROILER

2 tbsp	Dijon mustard	25 mL
2 tbsp	maple syrup	25 mL
2 tbsp	balsamic vinegar	25 mL
1 tbsp	chopped fresh rosemary (or 1 1/2 tsp [7 mL] dried)	15 mL
2	cloves garlic, minced	2
1/2 tsp	pepper	2 mL
8	lamb loin chops, 1 inch (2.5 cm) thick, trimmed (about 1 1/2 lbs [750 g])	8
	Salt	

1. In a shallow glass dish, combine mustard, maple syrup, balsamic vinegar, rosemary, garlic and pepper; add chops and turn to coat. Marinate at room temperature for 30 minutes, or cover and refrigerate, turning occasionally, for up to 8 hours. (Return meat to room temperature before cooking.)

2. Reserving the marinade, place chops on a greased grill or stovetop grill pan over medium-high heat; cook, basting with marinade, for 5 to 7 minutes on each side for medium-rare or desired doneness. (Or place on a broiler pan 4 inches (10 cm) below broiler, basting with marinade, for 5 to 7 minutes on each side for medium-rare or desired doneness.) Season with salt to taste.

Per serving	
Calories	209
Protein	23 g
Carbohydrates	10 g
Dietary Fiber	0 g
Fat - Total	8 g
Saturated Fat	3.5 g
Calcium	38 mg

SERVES 4

Fresh salmon doesn't need much to enhance it, but this simple-to-prepare pesto sauce keeps the fish extra moist and adds a burst of fresh flavor.

TIP

Swordfish, tuna or halibut steaks can be substituted for salmon.

Double the quantity of the pesto ingredients; use half to marinate fish and refrigerate the other half to use as a quick baste when grilling chicken, pork or lamb. Pesto can be refrigerated in a covered container for up to 1 week.

Simply Super Salmon with Lemon-Oregano Pesto

PREHEAT BARBECUE GRILL OR BROILER

1/2 cup	lightly packed parsley sprigs	125 mL
2 tbsp	chopped fresh oregano (or 2 tsp [10 mL] dried)	25 mL
1	clove garlic, minced	1
2 tbsp	olive oil	25 mL
2 tsp	grated lemon zest	10 mL
2 tbsp	freshly squeezed lemon juice	25 mL
	Salt and pepper	
1	salmon fillet, unskinned (about 1 1/4 lbs [625 g])	1

1. In a food processor or mini chopper, combine parsley, oregano, garlic, oil, lemon zest and juice; season with salt and pepper to taste. Purée until very smooth.

2. Arrange salmon in a shallow glass dish; coat both sides with pesto. Let stand at room temperature for 15 minutes or cover and refrigerate for up to 2 hours.

3. Place salmon skin-side down on greased grill over medium-high heat; cook 4 to 5 minutes for each side (allow 10 minutes per inch [2.5 cm] thickness) or until fish is opaque, and flakes easily with a fork. (Alternatively, arrange salmon on broiler pan 4 inches [10 cm] below broiler; cook for 5 minutes on each side or until fish is opaque and flakes easily with a fork.) Cut salmon into 4 portions and serve.

Per serving	
Calories	288
Protein	29 g
Carbohydrates	2 g
Dietary Fiber	0 g
Fat - Total	18 g
Saturated Fat	3.4 g
Calcium	40 mg

Microwave Sole with Orange-Ginger Sauce

8-INCH (2 L) SQUARE BAKING DISH

Fish and the microwave oven were meant for each other. Thanks to the steam-like cooking method of the microwave, fish cooks quickly yet stays beautifully moist.

TIP

I like to double this superb sweet-sour orange sauce and have it handy in the fridge to use as a quick baste when grilling chicken or pork. It also makes a great warm dipping sauce for chicken nuggets or fish sticks. Store sauce in a covered container in the refrigerator for up to 1 week.

White vinegar can be substituted for the milder rice vinegar, but increase brown sugar to 1 tbsp (15 mL).

Orange-Ginger Sauce

1/2 cup	orange juice	125 mL
1 tbsp	soya sauce	15 mL
1 tbsp	rice vinegar	15 mL
2 tsp	brown sugar	10 mL
1 1/2 tsp	cornstarch	7 mL
1 tsp	minced ginger root	5 mL
1 lb	sole, haddock or cod fillets	500 g
2	green onions, chopped	2

1. Orange-Ginger Sauce: In a glass measuring cup, combine orange juice, soya sauce, vinegar, brown sugar, cornstarch and ginger; stir until smooth. Microwave at High, stirring once, for 2 minutes or until sauce comes to a full boil and thickens. (Sauce should be quite thick.)

2. Pat fish dry with paper towels. Arrange in a single layer in baking dish. (For thin fillets, such as sole, turn tapered ends under.) Spread with sauce; sprinkle with green onions. Cover with microwave-safe plastic wrap; turn back one corner to vent. Microwave at High for 5 minutes or until fish turns opaque.

Per serving	
Calories	144
Protein	24 g
Carbohydrates	7 g
Dietary Fiber	0 g
Fat - Total	2 g
Saturated Fat	0.4 g
Calcium	33 mg

SERVES 4

Lemon-Teriyaki Halibut Kabobs

Make this tasty fish dish year-round on the barbecue or under the broiler. Remember when broiling foods to keep the oven door slightly ajar so that the main source of heat comes from the broiler. With the oven door closed, the entire oven heats up and foods tends to bake rather than broil.

TIP

This quick marinade can also be used for kabobs made with other fish such as salmon, or 1 lb (500 g) sea scallops or large raw shrimp, peeled and deveined with tails left on.

PREHEAT BARBECUE GRILL OR BROILER

1 1/4 lbs	halibut steaks, cut 1 inch (2.5 cm) thick	625 g
1/3 cup	teriyaki sauce	75 mL
1 tsp	grated lemon zest	5 mL
2 tbsp	freshly squeezed lemon juice	25 mL
1 tbsp	olive oil	15 mL
1	clove garlic, minced	1
2 tbsp	chopped green onions (green part only)	25 mL
	Lemon wedges	

1. Remove halibut skins and bones; cut into 1-inch (2.5 cm) cubes. Thread on 4 skewers. (If using wooden skewers, soak first in cold water for 30 minutes.) Arrange kabobs in shallow glass dish.

2. In a bowl combine teriyaki sauce, lemon zest and juice, oil and garlic; pour over skewers. Cover and marinate at room temperature for 15 to 30 minutes.

3. Reserving marinade, place skewers on greased grill over medium-high heat; cook, turning once, brushing with marinade, for 7 to 9 minutes or until fish flakes easily with a fork. (Alternatively, place on a broiler pan or rack set on a baking sheet; broil 4 inches (10 cm) from heat, turning once and basting with marinade, for 7 to 9 minutes or until fish flakes easily with a fork.) Transfer to a platter; garnish with chopped green onions and lemon wedges.

Per serving	
Calories	210
Protein	31 g
Carbohydrates	5 g
Dietary Fiber	0 g
Fat - Total	7 g
Saturated Fat	0.9 g
Calcium	77 mg

SERVES 4

Here's a no-fuss cooking technique for salmon. With this method you don't even need to turn the fillets over in the skillet. Serve the fish with steamed new potatoes as the perfect accompaniment. Try this method with other fillets such as halibut or snapper.

TIP

For the best flavor, use a top-quality olive oil. If substituting red wine vinegar for balsamic, sweeten with a pinch of sugar.

Pan-Roasted Salmon with Quick Tomato-Herb Sauce

2	ripe tomatoes, seeded and diced	2
2 tbsp	chopped fresh basil *or* chives	25 mL
2 tbsp	chopped parsley	25 mL
1 tbsp	balsamic vinegar *or* red wine vinegar	15 mL
2 tbsp	olive oil	25 mL
	Salt and pepper	
4	small salmon fillets *or* trout fillets (each about 5 oz [150 g])	4

1. In a bowl combine tomatoes, basil, parsley, vinegar and half of the oil; season with salt and pepper to taste.

2. Season fillets with salt and pepper. In a large nonstick skillet, heat remaining olive oil over medium-high heat; place fillets skin-side down in skillet. Cook for 2 minutes (do not turn). Reduce heat to medium-low, cover and cook for 4 to 5 minutes or until fish is opaque. Arrange on plates and top with tomato-herb sauce.

Per serving	
Calories	307
Protein	29 g
Carbohydrates	4 g
Dietary Fiber	1 g
Fat - Total	19 g
Saturated Fat	3.6 g
Calcium	25 mg

Pasta & Grains

SERVES 4

Spicy Shredded Beef with Angel Hair Pasta

Timing is everything when it comes to cooking pasta and preparing a stir-fry. Before you begin chopping the vegetables for this recipe, put a large pot of water on the stove to boil. The pasta takes just a few minutes to cook so don't add it to the boiling water until just after you brown the meat so both pasta and stir-fry will be ready at the same time.

TIP

Pork, chicken or firm tofu can replace the beef.

1/2 cup	chicken stock *or* water	125 mL
3 tbsp	soya sauce	45 mL
1 1/2 tsp	cornstarch	7 mL
12 oz	lean tender beef, such as sirloin, cut into very thin shreds	375 g
4 tsp	vegetable oil	20 mL
1 tbsp	minced ginger root	15 mL
2	cloves garlic, minced	2
1 tsp	Oriental chili paste *or* 1/2 tsp (2 mL) red pepper flakes	5 mL
2 cups	snow peas, trimmed and halved	500 mL
1	large red bell pepper, cut into thin 2-inch (5 cm) strips	1
4	green onions, chopped	4
8 oz	angel hair pasta	250 g

1. In a glass measuring cup, combine stock, soya sauce and cornstarch. Pat meat dry with paper towels.

2. In a wok or large nonstick skillet, heat half the oil over high heat. Add beef and stir-fry until browned; transfer to a plate. Add remaining oil to skillet. Add ginger, garlic and chili paste; cook, stirring, for 15 seconds. Stir in snow peas, red pepper and green onions; cook, stirring, for 1 minute. Add stock/soya mixture; cook until thickened. Return beef to skillet; cook, stirring, for 30 seconds.

3. Cook pasta in a large pot of boiling salted water until tender but firm. Drain well; return to pot. Add beef mixture and toss well. Serve immediately.

Per serving	
Calories	473
Protein	37 g
Carbohydrates	56 g
Dietary Fiber	6 g
Fat - Total	11 g
Saturated Fat	2.8 g
Calcium	60 mg

Fast-Lane Linguine with Chicken and Pesto

Here's a fast and easy recipe that streamlines preparation time by cooking the vegetables and the pasta together. Just throw the broccoli into the pot of boiling water for the last few minutes while the linguine is cooking. (This time-saver also works with other favorite pasta dishes.) Allow 1 to 2 minutes for quick-cooking veggies like snow peas and 2 to 3 minutes for longer-cooking veggies like carrots and broccoli.

TIP

Vary the flavor of this dish by substituting other herb pestos such as oregano or sun-dried tomato for the basil pesto. Every brand and type of pesto varies in strength; add the smaller amount as suggested in recipe and stir in more if needed.

1 tbsp	olive oil	15 mL
1 lb	skinless, boneless chicken breasts *or* turkey breasts, cut into thin strips	500 g
1/2 cup	chicken stock	125 mL
1/3 to 1/2 cup	basil pesto (store-bought or homemade)	75 to 125 mL
12 oz	linguine or other string pasta	375 g
4 cups	broccoli florets and peeled, chopped stems	1 L
1/3 cup	grated Parmesan cheese	75 mL
	Salt and pepper	

1. In a large nonstick skillet, heat oil over medium-high heat. Add chicken and cook, stirring, for 5 minutes or until no longer pink. Add stock and pesto; cook, stirring, for 1 minute or until heated through. Remove from heat.

2. Cook pasta in a large pot of boiling salted water until almost tender; add broccoli. Return to a boil; cook for 2 minutes or until broccoli is tender-crisp. Drain pasta and broccoli well; return to pot. Stir in chicken-pesto mixture; toss until well coated. Sprinkle with Parmesan cheese; season with salt and pepper to taste. Serve immediately.

Per serving	
Calories	654
Protein	44 g
Carbohydrates	73 g
Dietary Fiber	9 g
Fat - Total	20 g
Saturated Fat	5.6 g
Calcium	321 mg

Why do we love stir-frys? Recipes like this one are a huge time-saver for the home cook. Everything goes in one pot — meat, veggies and even pasta. Another plus: this recipe can be parceled into smaller portions that can be frozen for individual meals – just reheat in the microwave!

TIP

Whole grain pasta is used here, but any type of pasta such as vermicelli or spaghettini can be substituted.

Cut peppers into 2-inch (5 cm) strips.

Per serving	
Calories	354
Protein	28 g
Carbohydrates	51 g
Dietary Fiber	8 g
Fat - Total	6 g
Saturated Fat	1.1 g
Calcium	51 mg

Speedy Singapore Noodles with Pork and Peppers

1 lb	pork tenderloin	500 g
1 tbsp	vegetable oil	15 mL
1	leek, white and light green part only, cut into thin strips	1
2	large cloves garlic, minced	2
1	red bell pepper, cut into thin strips	1
1	yellow bell pepper, cut into thin strips	1
1	green bell pepper, cut into thin strips	1
3/4 cup	chicken stock	175 mL
1 tbsp	curry powder	15 mL
1/4 cup	bottled oyster sauce	50 mL
2 tsp	cornstarch	10 mL
12 oz	whole-wheat spaghetti	375 g
1/4 cup	chopped fresh coriander *or* parsley	50 mL

1. Cut pork into thin 2- by 1/4-inch (5 cm by 5 mm) strips. In a wok or large nonstick skillet, heat oil over high heat. Brown meat on all sides; remove to a plate and set aside. Add leek, garlic, pepper strips, chicken stock and curry powder to skillet; cover and cook for 2 minutes. Stir in oyster sauce.

2. In a small dish, dissolve cornstarch in 1 tbsp (15 mL) water; add to skillet along with pork. Bring sauce to boil; cook, stirring, for 1 to 2 minutes or until pork is heated through.

3. Cook pasta in a large pot of boiling salted water until tender but firm. Drain well. Return to pot; stir in meat mixture and coriander. Toss to coat well in sauce.

All-in-One Pasta and Chickpea Ragout

You only need one pot to prepare this dish. Even the dried pasta is added to the very same pot and cooked until tender in the vegetable-tomato sauce. Spoon into bowls and sprinkle with shredded Fontina or Parmesan cheese.

TIP

Keep single servings on hand in the freezer for quick microwave meals.

Add 8 oz (250 g) cubed or sliced smoked sausage such as kielbasa or ham along with chickpeas.

1 tbsp	olive oil	15 mL
1	medium onion, chopped	1
2	cloves garlic, minced	2
1	large green bell pepper, chopped	1
1 tsp	dried oregano	5 mL
1/2 tsp	dried basil	2 mL
1/2 tsp	salt	2 mL
1/4 tsp	red pepper flakes	1 mL
1	can (28 oz [796 mL]) tomatoes, chopped	1
1 cup	vegetable stock	250 mL
1 cup	elbow macaroni	250 mL
2	small zucchini, halved lengthwise and sliced	2
1	can (19 oz [540 mL]) chickpeas, rinsed and drained	1

1. In a Dutch oven or large saucepan, heat oil over medium heat. Add onion, garlic, pepper, oregano, basil, salt and red pepper flakes; cook, stirring, for 3 minutes or until vegetables are softened.

2. Add tomatoes and stock; bring to a boil. Reduce heat, cover and simmer, stirring occasionally, for 10 minutes. Stir in pasta; cover and cook for 5 minutes. Stir in zucchini and chickpeas; simmer for 5 to 7 minutes more or until pasta and zucchini are tender.

Per serving	
Calories	367
Protein	14 g
Carbohydrates	67 g
Dietary Fiber	11 g
Fat - Total	6 g
Saturated Fat	0.8 g
Calcium	141 mg

SERVES 6

With leftover cooked turkey, you can make a wonderful pasta dish that's great for company. To make the dish in advance, cook the sauce, cover and refrigerate. Boil the pasta, rinse under cold water and chill. Combine the cold sauce and pasta up to 4 hours before the dish goes in the oven. (This prevents the pasta from absorbing too much of the sauce.)

TIP

This casserole also works well with ham instead of turkey.

Per serving	
Calories	403
Protein	26 g
Carbohydrates	31 g
Dietary Fiber	2 g
Fat - Total	18 g
Saturated Fat	10.1 g
Calcium	201 mg

Company Turkey Tetrazzini

PREHEAT OVEN TO 350° F (180° C)
13- BY 9-INCH (3 L) BAKING DISH, BUTTERED

2 tbsp	butter	25 mL
8 oz	mushrooms, sliced	250 g
4	green onions, finely chopped	4
1 tsp	dried basil	5 mL
1/4 cup	all-purpose flour	50 mL
2 cups	turkey stock *or* chicken stock	500 mL
1/2 cup	whipping (35%) cream or light (10%) cream	125 mL
1/4 cup	medium-dry sherry	50 mL
2 cup	cubed cooked turkey *or* chicken	500 mL
2/3 cup	grated Parmesan cheese	150 mL
	Salt and pepper	
8 oz	broad egg noodles	250 g

1. In a large saucepan, melt butter over medium-high heat. Add mushrooms, green onions and basil; cook for 4 minutes or until softened. In a bowl, blend flour with 1/3 cup (75 mL) of the stock to make a smooth paste; stir in remaining stock. Pour into saucepan; bring to a boil, stirring, until thickened. Add cream, sherry and turkey; cook over medium heat for 2 to 3 minutes or until heated through. Remove from heat. Stir in half the Parmesan cheese; season with salt and pepper to taste.

2. Cook noodles in a large pot of boiling salted water until almost tender but firm. Drain well. Return to pot; add turkey mixture and toss to coat well. Spoon into prepared baking dish. Sprinkle with remaining Parmesan cheese. Bake for 30 to 35 minutes or until heated through. (If refrigerated, cook 10 minutes more or until piping hot in center.)

SERVES 6 TO 8

Penne with Red Peppers and Three Cheeses

I like to have leftovers of this creamy pasta dish on hand because it's perfect for reheating later in the week. This pasta is creamy – but don't be deceived. Thanks to low-fat ricotta and feta cheese, (similar in fat content to part-skim mozzarella), the fat and calories are kept in check.

TIP

Extras also freeze well; add about 2 tbsp (25 mL) water when reheating.

4 tsp	olive oil	20 mL
2	large red bell peppers, cut into 2-inch (5 cm) thin strips	2
3	cloves garlic, minced	3
1 tbsp	dried oregano	15 mL
1/2 tsp	red pepper flakes	2 mL
1 cup	low-fat ricotta cheese	250 mL
1 cup	crumbled feta cheese	250 mL
1/2 cup	grated Parmesan cheese	125 mL
1 lb	penne or other tube-shaped pasta	500 g
1/3 cup	chopped parsley	75 mL
	Salt and pepper	

1. In large nonstick skillet, heat oil over medium heat. Add bell peppers, garlic, oregano and red pepper flakes; cook, stirring, for 5 minutes or until softened. Remove from heat.

2. In a food processor, combine ricotta, feta and Parmesan; purée until smooth.

3. Cook pasta in a large pot of boiling salted water until tender but firm. Reserve 1 cup (250 mL) of the hot cooking liquid. Drain pasta; return to pot over low heat. Stir in cheese mixture along with enough of the hot cooking liquid to make a creamy sauce. Stir in vegetable mixture and parsley; season with salt and pepper to taste.

Per serving (8)	
Calories	334
Protein	15 g
Carbohydrates	42 g
Dietary Fiber	2 g
Fat - Total	12 g
Saturated Fat	6 g
Calcium	287 mg

Spaghetti with Quick Garlic Tomato Sauce

Even when my pantry is almost empty, chances are I'll have a can of tomatoes and dried pasta on hand to whip up this easy supper dish.

TIP

Improvise if you don't have any fresh herbs by using 1 tsp (5 mL) each dried basil and dried oregano for the fresh basil and parsley.

VARIATION

Quick Creamy Tomato Sauce

Instead of the traditional accompaniment of freshly grated Parmesan cheese, toss hot pasta with 5 oz (150 g) creamy goat cheese, soft Brie or Gorgonzola, rind removed and cut into small pieces.

2 tbsp	olive oil	25 mL
3	cloves garlic thinly sliced, then coarsely chopped	3
1/4 tsp	red pepper flakes	1 mL
1	can (28 oz [796 mL]) plum tomatoes, chopped	1
	Salt and pepper	
Pinch	granulated sugar	Pinch
12 oz	spaghetti	375 g
2 tbsp	chopped parsley	25 mL
2 tbsp	chopped fresh basil *or* chives	25 mL

1. In a large saucepan, heat oil over medium heat; stir in garlic and red pepper flakes. Reduce heat to low; cook, stirring, for 1 minute or until garlic is light golden. (Do not let garlic brown or sauce will be bitter.) Add tomatoes; season with salt, pepper and sugar to taste. Bring to a boil, reduce heat and simmer, partially covered, stirring occasionally, for 15 minutes.

2. Cook pasta in a large pot of boiling salted water until tender but firm. Drain well; return to pot. Add tomato sauce, parsley and basil; toss well. Adjust seasoning with salt and pepper. Serve immediately.

Per serving (6)	
Calories	292
Protein	9 g
Carbohydrates	52 g
Dietary Fiber	4 g
Fat - Total	6 g
Saturated Fat	0.8 g
Calcium	59 mg

Fast Fusilli with Mushrooms and Peas

I like to use fusilli in this recipe because the sauce clings nicely to the corkscrew-shaped pasta but feel free to use whatever pasta you have in your pantry.

TIP

You can make this 5-minute pasta sauce the day ahead and refrigerate. Reheat on stovetop or microwave before tossing with hot cooked pasta.

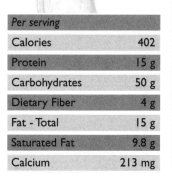

2 tsp	butter	10 mL
2 cups	sliced mushrooms	500 mL
2	green onions, chopped	2
4 oz	cream cheese flavored with herbs and garlic	125 g
1 cup	frozen peas	250 mL
1/2 cup	milk	125 mL
1/3 cup	grated Parmesan cheese	75 mL
8 oz	fusilli, penne or other tube-shaped pasta	250 g
	Salt and pepper	

1. In a large saucepan, melt butter over medium heat. Add mushrooms and green onions; cook, stirring, for 3 minutes or until softened. Add flavored cream cheese, peas, milk and Parmesan; cook, stirring, for 2 minutes or until piping hot.

2. Cook pasta in a large pot of boiling salted water until tender but firm. Drain well. Stir into mushroom mixture; toss to coat well. Season with salt and pepper to taste. Serve immediately.

Per serving	
Calories	402
Protein	15 g
Carbohydrates	50 g
Dietary Fiber	4 g
Fat - Total	15 g
Saturated Fat	9.8 g
Calcium	213 mg

Toss this luxurious basil and walnut sauce with bow ties or any other interesting pasta shapes and get ready to entertain. It takes only 5 minutes to make and can be prepared a few hours ahead and reheated over low heat just before serving.

TIP

Walnuts can go rancid quickly and impart a very bitter taste that can ruin a recipe. Rely on California walnuts for best quality. To maintain freshness, store walnuts as well as other nuts – such as pecans, hazelnuts and pine nuts – in a covered container in the fridge or freezer.

Per serving	
Calories	427
Protein	15 g
Carbohydrates	52 g
Dietary Fiber	3 g
Fat - Total	18 g
Saturated Fat	8.4 g
Calcium	215 mg

Creamy Bow Ties with Basil

1 tbsp	butter	15 mL
4	green onions, chopped	4
2	cloves garlic, finely chopped	2
1/4 cup	finely chopped walnuts	50 mL
1 cup	light (10 %) cream	250 mL
1/3 cup	grated Parmesan cheese	75 mL
8 oz	bow tie pasta	250 g
1/3 cup	chopped fresh basil	75 mL
	Salt and pepper	

1. In a large saucepan, melt butter over medium heat. Add green onions, garlic and walnuts; cook, stirring, for 2 minutes or until onions are softened. Stir in cream and Parmesan. Keep warm over low heat; do not let mixture boil.

2. Cook pasta in a large pot of boiling salted water until tender but firm. Drain well; add to cream sauce along with basil and toss to coat. Season with salt and pepper to taste. Serve immediately.

**SERVES 4 AS
A MAIN COURSE OR
6 AS A SIDE DISH**

Packed with bold flavors, this tasty pasta dish goes well with salad greens such as radicchio, endive and arugula. I also like to serve it as a side dish with grilled sausages.

TIP

Place a large pot of water on the stovetop, then assemble and prepare all the ingredients for the sauce. As soon as the pasta goes into the boiling water, start cooking the sauce. Both pasta and sauce should be ready at about the same time.

Speedy Spaghettini with Artichokes and Red Peppers

2 tbsp	olive oil	25 mL
1	medium red onion, cut lengthwise into thin strips	1
4	cloves garlic, minced	4
1 1/2 tsp	dried oregano	7 mL
1/2 tsp	red pepper flakes	2 mL
1	can (14 oz [398 mL]) artichoke hearts, drained and cut into wedges	1
3/4 cup	bottled roasted red peppers, rinsed, patted dry and cut into strips	175 mL
1/2 cup	dry-cured small black olives	125 mL
1/2 cup	chicken stock *or* vegetable stock	125 mL
12 oz	spaghettini	375 g
1/3 cup	chopped parsley	75 mL
1/2 cup	grated Romano cheese *or* Parmesan cheese	125 mL

1. In a large nonstick skillet, heat oil over medium heat. Add onion, garlic, oregano and red pepper flakes; cook, stirring often, for 2 minutes or until softened. Add artichokes, red pepper strips, olives and stock; cook, stirring often, for 4 minutes.

2. Cook pasta in a large pot of boiling salted water until tender but firm. Drain pasta well; return to pot. Stir in vegetable mixture, parsley and Romano cheese; toss well. Serve immediately.

Per serving (6)	
Calories	452
Protein	19 g
Carbohydrates	58 g
Dietary Fiber	8 g
Fat - Total	17 g
Saturated Fat	2.2 g
Calcium	202 mg

Toss this pesto with hot cooked pasta for a fast dinner or swirl it into soup for a wonderful burst of flavor.

TIP

If fresh basil is unavailable, increase parsley to 1 cup (250 mL) and add 1 tbsp (15 mL) dried basil.

Pesto can be stored in covered container in refrigerator for up to 5 days or frozen for up to 1 month.

Penne with Sun-Dried Tomato Pesto

Sun-Dried Tomato Pesto

1/2 cup	sun-dried tomatoes	125 mL
1/2 cup	packed fresh basil	125 mL
1/2 cup	packed fresh parsley	125 mL
1	large clove garlic	1
1/3 cup	vegetable stock	75 mL
2 tbsp	olive oil	25 mL
1/3 cup	grated Parmesan cheese	75 mL
1/2 tsp	pepper	2 mL
12 oz	penne	375 g
1/3 cup	grated Parmesan cheese	75 mL

1. Pesto: In a bowl cover sun-dried tomatoes with boiling water; let stand 10 minutes or until softened. Drain and pat dry; chop coarsely.
2. In a food processor, combine rehydrated tomatoes, basil, parsley and garlic. With motor running, add stock and oil in a stream. Stir in Parmesan cheese and pepper.
3. Cook pasta in a large pot of boiling salted water until tender but firm. Set aside 3/4 cup (175 mL) pasta cooking liquid. Drain pasta well; return to pot. Stir hot pasta cooking liquid into pesto; pour over pasta and toss well. Place on serving plates; sprinkle with additional Parmesan cheese.

Per serving (6)	
Calories	280
Protein	10 g
Carbohydrates	43 g
Dietary Fiber	3 g
Fat - Total	7 g
Saturated Fat	1.8 g
Calcium	109 mg

Easy One-Pot Macaroni and Cheese

Why resort to pre-packaged macaroni dinners when it's so easy to make this popular dish from scratch?

TIP

For a speedy, meal-in-one dinner add 3 to 4 cups (750 mL to 1 L) small broccoli florets to the pot of boiling pasta for the last 3 minutes of cooking; remove from heat when broccoli is tender-crisp.

To reheat leftovers on the stovetop or in the microwave, stir in additional milk until sauce is creamy.

2 tbsp	all-purpose flour	25 mL
1 1/2 cups	milk	375 mL
1 1/2 cups	shredded Cheddar cheese	375 mL
1/4 cup	grated Parmesan cheese	50 mL
1 tsp	Dijon mustard	5 mL
	Salt and cayenne pepper	
2 cups	elbow macaroni	500 mL

1. In a large saucepan, whisk flour with 1/4 cup (50 mL) of the milk to make a smooth paste; stir in remaining milk until smooth. Place over medium heat; cook, stirring, until mixture comes to a boil and thickens. Reduce heat to low; stir in cheeses and mustard. Cook, stirring, until melted. Season with salt and a pinch of cayenne pepper to taste; keep warm.

2. Cook pasta in a large pot of boiling salted water until tender but firm. Drain well; stir into cheese mixture. Cook for 1 minute or until sauce coats the pasta. Serve immediately.

Per serving	
Calories	450
Protein	23 g
Carbohydrates	46 g
Dietary Fiber	2 g
Fat - Total	19 g
Saturated Fat	11.5 g
Calcium	515 mg

Nutritionists recommend adding more grain to our diets. Here's a dish to serve to your family that is not only great-tasting, but wholesome besides.

TIP

Other nuts, such as skinned hazelnuts or unblanched almonds, can be substituted for the walnuts.

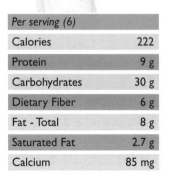

Mushroom Barley Pilaf

1 tbsp	butter	15 mL
2 cups	sliced mushrooms	500 mL
1	small onion, chopped	1
1/2 tsp	dried thyme *or* marjoram	2 mL
1 cup	pearl barley, rinsed	250 mL
2 1/2 cups	chicken stock *or* vegetable stock	625 mL
1/3 cup	finely chopped walnuts or pecans	75 mL
1/4 cup	grated Parmesan cheese	50 mL
2 tbsp	chopped parsley	25 mL
	Salt and pepper	

1. In a medium saucepan, heat butter over medium heat. Add mushrooms, onion and thyme; cook, stirring, for 5 minutes or until softened.

2. Stir in barley and stock; bring to a boil. Reduce heat, cover and simmer, stirring occasionally and adding more stock if necessary, for 30 minutes or until barley is tender.

3. Stir in walnuts, Parmesan and parsley; season with salt and pepper to taste.

Per serving (6)	
Calories	222
Protein	9 g
Carbohydrates	30 g
Dietary Fiber	6 g
Fat - Total	8 g
Saturated Fat	2.7 g
Calcium	85 mg

SERVES 4

Rice with Snow Peas and Red Pepper

Here's a colorful side dish that's a snap to prepare because the vegetables are cooked with the rice.

TIP

Serve this tasty side-dish with chicken or pork. Substitute brown rice for the white rice; increase stock to 2 1/2 cups (625 mL). Increase cooking time to 40 minutes.

VARIATIONS

Instead of snow peas and red peppers, substitute 2 cups (500 mL) small broccoli florets and 2 carrots, thinly sliced on the diagonal, or 1 lb (500 g) asparagus, ends trimmed and cut on the diagonal into 1 1/2-inch (4 cm) pieces.

2 cups	chicken stock	500 mL
2 tbsp	soya sauce	25 mL
1 1/2 tsp	minced ginger root (or 1/2 tsp [2 mL] ground ginger)	7 mL
1	clove garlic, minced	1
1 cup	long-grain white rice	250 mL
2 cups	snow peas, cut into 1-inch (2.5 cm) diagonal pieces (about 8 oz [250 g])	500 mL
Half	red bell pepper, diced	Half
3	green onions, chopped	3
1 tsp	toasted sesame oil (optional)	5 mL

1. In a medium saucepan, combine stock, soya sauce, ginger and garlic; bring to a boil. Stir in rice; reduce heat to low, cover and simmer for 20 minutes or until rice is just tender.
2. Add snow peas, red pepper and green onions. Cook, covered, for 5 minutes more or until vegetables are tender-crisp. Stir in sesame oil, if using.

Per serving	
Calories	250
Protein	9 g
Carbohydrates	49 g
Dietary Fiber	3 g
Fat - Total	1 g
Saturated Fat	0.4 g
Calcium	69 mg

With a vegetarian in the family, I count on this Indian-inspired dish with its bold seasonings as a reliable main-course dish. A bowlful makes a quick and easy supper.

TIP

For a meat-lover's version of this dish, add chopped leftover roast lamb, roast beef or baked ham for the last 10 minutes of cooking.

Quick Curried Lentils

1 tbsp	vegetable oil	15 mL
1	medium onion, chopped	1
3	cloves garlic, finely chopped	3
1 tbsp	minced ginger root (or 1 tsp [5 mL] ground ginger)	15 mL
2 tsp	ground cumin	10 mL
1 tsp	ground coriander	5 mL
1 cup	green lentils, washed and sorted	250 mL
1	can (19 oz [540 mL]) tomatoes, chopped	1
1 1/2 cups	vegetable stock *or* chicken stock	375 mL
1/3 cup	chopped fresh coriander *or* parsley	75 mL
	Salt and pepper	

1. In a large saucepan, heat oil over medium heat. Add onion, garlic, ginger, cumin and coriander; cook, stirring, for 3 minutes or until softened.
2. Add lentils, tomatoes and stock. Bring to a boil; reduce heat, cover and simmer for 35 minutes or until lentils are tender. Stir in coriander; season with salt and pepper to taste.

Per serving (6)	
Calories	152
Protein	9 g
Carbohydrates	24 g
Dietary Fiber	9 g
Fat - Total	3 g
Saturated Fat	0.2 g
Calcium	61 mg

ONE-POT ITALIAN SAUSAGES BRAISED WITH POTATOES (PAGE 83)
OVERLEAF: FARMHOUSE APPLE PIE (PAGE 170)

Last-Minute Moroccan-Style Couscous

Here's a colorful side dish that's ready in 10 minutes. What could be more simple?

TIP

For a simpler version, omit the dried fruits and nuts.

1 1/2 cups	chicken stock	375 mL
1/2 tsp	ground cumin	2 mL
1 cup	couscous	250 mL
2	green onions, finely chopped	2
1/3 cup	raisins *or* slivered dried apricots	75 mL
3 tbsp	slivered almonds *or* shelled pistachios *or* pecans	45 mL

1. In a small saucepan, bring chicken stock and cumin to a boil. Stir in couscous, green onions, raisins and almonds. Remove from heat; cover and let stand 5 minutes. Fluff with a fork and serve.

Per serving	
Calories	255
Protein	9 g
Carbohydrates	45 g
Dietary Fiber	4 g
Fat - Total	4 g
Saturated Fat	0.4 g
Calcium	38 mg

◄ SPEEDY SINGAPORE NOODLES WITH PORK AND PEPPERS (PAGE 116)

This makes a wonderful main-course dish, perfect for a potluck or buffet supper. It can also double as a side dish to serve with grilled lamb or chicken.

TIP

To thaw frozen spinach, place in a covered casserole and microwave at High for 5 minutes, stirring once.

To cook rice, bring 2 cups (500 mL) water to a boil in a medium saucepan; add 1 cup (250 mL) white long grain rice and 1/2 tsp (2 mL) salt. Return to a boil; reduce heat to low, cover and simmer for 20 minutes. If using brown rice, increase water to 2 1/2 cups (625 mL) and increase cooking time to 40 to 45 minutes. Makes 3 cups (750 mL) rice.

Greek Rice and Spinach Bake

PREHEAT OVEN TO 350° F (180° C)
8-INCH (2 L) SQUARE BAKING DISH, BUTTERED

1 tbsp	butter	15 mL
1	pkg (10 oz [300 g]) frozen chopped spinach, defrosted and squeezed dry	1
1	small onion, finely chopped	1
3	eggs	3
3/4 cup	milk	175 mL
1/4 tsp	ground nutmeg	1 mL
3 cups	cooked white or brown rice	750 mL
3/4 cup	finely crumbled feta cheese	175 mL
2 tbsp	chopped fresh dill (or 1 tsp [5 mL] dried)	25 mL
2 tbsp	fine dry bread crumbs	25 mL
2 tbsp	grated Parmesan cheese	25 mL

1. In a large nonstick skillet, heat butter over medium heat. Add spinach and onion; cook, stirring, for 4 minutes or until tender. Let cool slightly.

2. In a large bowl, beat eggs with milk and nutmeg; add rice, feta and dill. Stir in spinach mixture; spread in baking dish.

3. In a small bowl, combine bread crumbs and Parmesan cheese; sprinkle over spinach mixture. Bake for 35 to 40 minutes or until top is lightly browned and center is set. Cut into squares and serve.

Per serving (6)	
Calories	252
Protein	11 g
Carbohydrates	29 g
Dietary Fiber	2 g
Fat - Total	10 g
Saturated Fat	5.7 g
Calcium	241 mg

Traditional paella is made in a wide shallow pan, but today's nonstick skillet makes a very good substitute and reduces the amount of oil needed for this dish. If you don't have a skillet with an oven-proof handle, wrap the handle in a double layer of aluminum foil to protect it from the oven heat.

TIP

Try a variety of different vegetables, including bite-sized pieces of broccoli, cauliflower, asparagus, green beans, bell peppers and zucchini.

Spanish Vegetable Paella

PREHEAT OVEN TO 375° F (190° C)

4 cups	assorted prepared vegetables (see Tip, at left)	1 L
3 1/2 cups	chicken stock *or* vegetable stock	875 mL
1/4 tsp	saffron threads, crushed	1 mL
Pinch	red pepper flakes	Pinch
	Salt	
2 tbsp	olive oil	25 mL
4	green onions, chopped	4
3	large cloves garlic, finely chopped	3
1 1/2 cups	short grain white rice such as Arborio	375 mL

1. Cook vegetables (except peppers and zucchini) in a saucepan of boiling, lightly salted water, for 1 minute. Rinse under cold water to chill; drain well.

2. In the same saucepan, bring stock to a boil. Add saffron and red pepper flakes; season with salt to taste. Keep warm.

3. In a large nonstick skillet, heat oil over medium-high heat. Add green onions and garlic; cook, stirring, for 1 minute. Add vegetables to skillet; cook, stirring often, for 4 minutes or until lightly colored. Stir in rice and hot stock mixture. Reduce heat so rice cooks at a gentle boil: cook, uncovered, without stirring, for 10 minutes or until most of the liquid is absorbed.

4. Cover skillet with lid or foil. (If skillet handle is not ovenproof, wrap in double layer of foil.) Bake for 15 minutes or until all liquid is absorbed and rice is tender. Remove; let stand, covered, for 5 minutes before serving.

Per serving (6)	
Calories	221
Protein	7 g
Carbohydrates	35 g
Dietary Fiber	3 g
Fat - Total	6 g
Saturated Fat	0.9 g
Calcium	30 mg

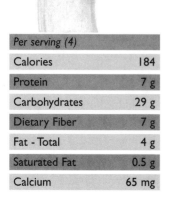

Canned beans are fast food for
vegetarians like my daughter
who is in college and calls this
her mainstay. Here's how to
turn a simple can of beans into
a tasty side dish or a terrific
main course.

TIP

Instead of fresh tomatoes, use
1 1/2 cups (375 mL) canned
tomatoes.

Mediterranean White Beans with Tomatoes

1 tbsp	olive oil	15 mL
1	small onion, chopped	1
2	cloves garlic, minced	2
1	green bell pepper, chopped	1
1/2 tsp	dried oregano	2 mL
1/4 tsp	dried thyme	1 mL
2	tomatoes, seeded and chopped	2
1 tbsp	balsamic vinegar	15 mL
1	can (19 oz [540 mL]) white kidney beans *or* Romano beans, rinsed and drained	1
	Salt and hot pepper sauce	

1. In a large saucepan, heat oil over medium heat. Add onion, garlic, green pepper, oregano and thyme; cook, stirring, for 2 minutes or until vegetables are softened. Add tomatoes and vinegar. (Depending on juiciness of fresh tomatoes, you may need to add 2 tbsp [25 mL] water to prevent mixture from sticking.)

2. Reduce heat, cover and simmer for 5 minutes or until vegetables are tender. Add beans and cook for 3 minutes or until heated through. Season with salt and hot pepper sauce to taste. Serve warm or at room temperature.

Per serving (4)	
Calories	184
Protein	7 g
Carbohydrates	29 g
Dietary Fiber	7 g
Fat - Total	4 g
Saturated Fat	0.5 g
Calcium	65 mg

Spiced Basmati Rice

This is my family's favorite rice dish. They love the taste of basmati rice, accented in this dish with ginger and a hint of cinnamon.

TIP

Rinsing and soaking the basmati rice removes excess starch and produces a less sticky, fluffier rice when cooked. Serve with grilled chicken or fish, or a curried lentil dish along with a steamed vegetable such as broccoli.

1 1/2 cups	basmati rice	375 mL
1 tbsp	butter	15 mL
1	small onion, finely chopped	1
1 tbsp	minced ginger root	15 mL
1	cinnamon stick, broken into 2 pieces	1
1	bay leaf	1
2 1/4 cups	water	550 mL
1 tsp	salt	5 mL
2 tbsp	chopped fresh coriander *or* parsley (optional)	25 mL

1. Place rice in sieve; rinse under cold water. Transfer to a bowl; add water to cover. Let soak for 15 minutes. Drain.

2. In a medium saucepan, melt butter over medium heat. Add onion, ginger, cinnamon and bay leaf; cook, stirring, for 2 minutes or until onion is softened. Add rice, water, and salt; bring to a boil. Reduce heat to low, cover and simmer for 10 minutes or until water is absorbed. Remove pan from heat; fluff with a fork. Let stand, uncovered, for 5 minutes. Remove cinnamon stick and bay leaf; sprinkle with coriander, if using.

Per serving	
Calories	207
Protein	4 g
Carbohydrates	42 g
Dietary Fiber	1 g
Fat - Total	3 g
Saturated Fat	1.4 g
Calcium	16 mg

SERVES 4

In-a-Jiffy Black Bean Chili with Salsa

Beat the clock with this warming one-pot chili for an easy vegetarian supper. Any kind of canned beans, such as chickpeas or kidney beans, can be used. Since canned beans and salsa tend to be salty, there's no need for any extra salt.

TIP

Medium salsa gives a burst of heat. For a tamer chili, use mild salsa.

For a meat-based chili, add 1 cup (250 mL) diced cooked ham or smoked sausage (such as kielbasa) along with beans.

2 tsp	vegetable oil	10 mL
1	small onion, finely chopped	1
2	cloves garlic, finely chopped	2
1	large green bell pepper, diced	1
2 tsp	chili powder	10 mL
1 tsp	dried oregano	5 mL
1/2 tsp	ground cumin	2 mL
1 1/2 cups	bottled mild or medium salsa	375 mL
3/4 cup	water *or* vegetable stock (approximate)	175 mL
1	can (19 oz [540 mL]) black beans, rinsed and drained	1
1 cup	frozen or canned corn kernels	250 mL

1. In a large saucepan, heat oil over medium heat. Add onion, garlic, green pepper, chili powder, oregano and cumin; cook, stirring, for 3 minutes or until softened.

2. Add salsa and water. Bring to a boil; reduce heat, cover and simmer for 5 minutes. Stir in black beans and corn; simmer, covered, for 5 minutes or until piping hot.

Per serving	
Calories	218
Protein	11 g
Carbohydrates	38 g
Dietary Fiber	12 g
Fat - Total	4 g
Saturated Fat	0.3 g
Calcium	114 mg

VEGETABLES & SALADS

Terrific Thai Chicken Salad

Thai food has become the rage in North America. Many supermarkets now stock a wide variety of Asian food products including fish sauce and chili paste. Fish sauce, called *nam pla*, is a salty brown seasoning that is the backbone of Thai cooking.

TIP

Use 3 tbsp (45 mL) soya sauce instead of fish sauce, if desired.

Spaghettini, cooked according to package directions, can be substituted for the rice vermicelli.

4	skinned chicken breasts, bone-in	4
4 oz	rice vermicelli	125 g
Half	medium seedless cucumber, cut into thin 2-inch (5 cm) strips	Half
1	large red bell pepper, cut into thin 2-inch (5 cm) strips	1
1/4 cup	chopped fresh basil *or* mint	50 mL

Dressing

1/4 cup	fish sauce	50 mL
3 tbsp	freshly squeezed lime juice	45 mL
2 tbsp	packed brown sugar	25 mL
1 tbsp	minced ginger root	15 mL
1	clove garlic, minced	1
1/2 tsp	Oriental chili paste *or* hot pepper sauce	2 mL
	Lettuce	
	Additional basil or mint	

1. In a large saucepan, bring 2 cups (500 mL) lightly salted water to a boil; reduce heat to medium-low. Add chicken; poach for 13 to 15 minutes, turning halfway through, until no longer pink inside. Let cool in broth. Debone chicken; cut into 1 1/2-inch (4 cm) strips.

2. In a bowl cover vermicelli with hot water; let stand 3 minutes or until softened. Drain well. In a bowl combine chicken, vermicelli, cucumber, red pepper and basil.

3. Dressing: In a bowl combine fish sauce, lime juice, brown sugar, ginger, garlic and chili paste. Just before serving, pour over chicken mixture; toss well. Serve salad on platter lined with lettuce; garnish with additional basil.

Per serving	
Calories	304
Protein	32 g
Carbohydrates	36 g
Dietary Fiber	2 g
Fat - Total	3 g
Saturated Fat	0.9 g
Calcium	50 mg

There are so many wonderful mushroom varieties in supermarkets these days. Feel free to use any mushroom combination, depending on what's available, when you make this earthy starter or luncheon salad. Select apple varieties such as Cortland or Granny Smith, which resist browning when sliced.

TIP

Most produce stores sell mixes of exotic greens, but you can make your own mixture using radicchio, arugula and oak leaf lettuces. Instead of goat cheese, use brie or a creamy blue cheese. Toast walnuts in a 350° F (180° C) oven for 7 to 9 minutes.

Per serving	
Calories	388
Protein	12 g
Carbohydrates	37 g
Dietary Fiber	5 g
Fat - Total	24 g
Saturated Fat	7.1 g
Calcium	127 mg

Warm Mushroom and Goat Cheese Salad

6 cups	Mesclun or mixed salad greens	1.5 L
1	large apple, quartered and cored	1
1	log (5 oz [150 g]) goat cheese, cut into 8 slices	1
2 tbsp	olive oil	25 mL
8 oz	cremini (small brown mushrooms), thickly sliced	250 g
4 oz	assorted mushrooms, such as oyster, shiitake and porcini, thickly sliced	125 g
1/2 cup	chopped green onions	125 mL
1/4 cup	honey	50 mL
1/4 cup	cider vinegar	50 mL
1/4 tsp	salt	1 mL
1/4 tsp	pepper	1 mL
1/2 cup	coarsely chopped toasted walnuts	125 mL

1. Divide salad greens among 4 plates. Cut apple quarters into 8 thin slices; arrange in a circle in middle of each plate. Place 2 slices goat cheese in center of each circle. (Can be done shortly before serving, covered and refrigerated.)

2. In a large nonstick skillet, heat oil over medium-high heat. Cook mushrooms, stirring, for 3 to 5 minutes or until tender. Add green onions, honey, vinegar, salt and pepper; cook, stirring, for 15 seconds or until hot. Remove from heat. Spoon warm mushroom mixture over salad greens. Sprinkle with walnuts. Serve immediately.

Make-Ahead Vegetable Noodle Salad with Spicy Peanut Dressing

Add whatever vegetables you have in the fridge to this all-purpose salad. Colorful choices include sliced zucchini, cubes of bell pepper, thinly sliced or grated carrots, broccoli and cauliflower florets.

TIP

If desired, toss in thinly sliced grilled steak or strips of boneless cooked chicken breast along with the noodle-vegetable mixture.

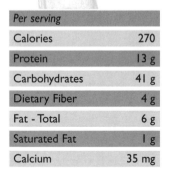

8 oz	spaghetti, broken into 3-inch (8 cm) lengths	250 g
4 cups	assorted chopped vegetables	1 L
3	green onions, chopped	3

Dressing

1/4 cup	light peanut butter	50 mL
2 tbsp	soya sauce	25 mL
2 tbsp	rice vinegar	25 mL
1 tbsp	toasted sesame oil	15 mL
2 tsp	packed brown sugar	10 mL
1 tbsp	minced ginger root	15 mL
1	clove garlic, minced	1
1/2 tsp	Oriental chili paste *or* hot pepper sauce to taste	2 mL
1/3 cup	chopped fresh coriander	75 mL

1. Cook pasta in a large pot of boiling salted water until tender but firm. Rinse under cold water to chill; drain well. Place in a serving bowl; add vegetables and green onions.

2. Dressing: In a bowl whisk together peanut butter, soya sauce, vinegar, sesame oil, brown sugar, ginger, garlic and chili paste. Pour over pasta mixture; toss well to coat. Sprinkle with coriander.

Per serving	
Calories	270
Protein	13 g
Carbohydrates	41 g
Dietary Fiber	4 g
Fat - Total	6 g
Saturated Fat	1 g
Calcium	35 mg

Simply Elegant Grilled Salmon and Romaine Salad

You won't believe how easy it is to make this elegant grilled salmon on a bed of fresh-tossed greens. Count on spending no more than 30 minutes to prepare this meal-in-one dish, ideal for a patio supper with friends. The dressing, made quickly in the food processor, does double duty as a marinade for the salmon and a dressing for the salad.

TIP

You can still make this salad after barbecue season or even when it's raining. Cook the salmon on a stove-top grill pan or place on a broiler pan 4 inches (10 cm) below preheated broiler for the same cooking time.

Dressing

2 cups	lightly packed parsley	500 mL
1/4 cup	orange juice	50 mL
2 tbsp	olive oil	25 mL
2 tbsp	red wine vinegar	25 mL
1 tbsp	Dijon mustard	15 mL
1/2 tsp	salt	1 mL
1/2 tsp	pepper	1 mL
1	clove garlic, minced	1
1 tsp	grated orange zest	5 mL

Salad

1	salmon fillet, unskinned (about 1 1/4 lbs [625 g])	1
8 cups	torn romaine lettuce	2 L
2 cups	halved cherry tomatoes	500 mL
Half	medium seedless cucumber, halved lengthwise and sliced	Half

1. Dressing: In a food processor, combine parsley, orange juice, oil, vinegar, mustard, salt and pepper; process until parsley is very finely chopped. Transfer to a glass bowl. Stir in garlic and orange zest. Arrange salmon fillet in shallow baking dish; spread with 1/4 cup (50 mL) of the dressing. Let marinate at room temperature for 15 minutes, turning occasionally.

2. Place salmon skin-side down on greased grill over medium-high heat; cook, turning once halfway through, for 10 minutes per inch (2.5 cm) thickness or until fish flakes when tested with fork and flesh is opaque. Remove and let stand for 5 minutes. Remove skin; cut into 4 portions.

3. In a large bowl, combine romaine, cherry tomatoes and cucumber. Pour over remaining dressing; toss to coat lightly. Divide salad among serving plates; top with salmon. Serve immediately.

Per serving	
Calories	373
Protein	32 g
Carbohydrates	12 g
Dietary Fiber	4 g
Fat - Total	22 g
Saturated Fat	4 g
Calcium	120 mg

Spinach, Mushroom and Carrot Salad

This party salad is not complicated to make, neither is it expensive to prepare. But the flavors make it special enough to serve for company — with tangy lime juice, mustard and cumin balancing the sweetness of raisins and carrots.

TIP

This colorful salad can be made up to 4 hours ahead and refrigerated. Add the dressing and toss just before serving. Use 3/4 tsp (4 mL) dried *fines herbes* instead of cumin, if desired.

8 cups	coarsely chopped fresh spinach (about 1 10 oz [300 g] bag), stemmed	2 L
1 1/2 cups	sliced mushrooms	375 mL
2 cups	peeled shredded carrots	500 mL
1 1/2 cups	seedless cucumbers, halved lengthwise and sliced	375 mL
1	small red onion, thinly sliced	1
1/3 cup	dark raisins	75 mL

Dressing

1/4 cup	olive oil	50 mL
2 tbsp	freshly squeezed lime juice	25 mL
1 tbsp	honey	15 mL
2 tsp	Dijon mustard	10 mL
3/4 tsp	ground cumin	4 mL
1	clove garlic, minced	1
1/2 tsp	salt	2 mL
1/4 tsp	pepper	1 mL

1. In a serving bowl, layer one-third of the shredded spinach, all the sliced mushrooms, another one-third of the spinach, all the shredded carrots, then remaining spinach. Layer cucumbers, onion and raisins over top. Cover and refrigerate up to 4 hours.

2. Dressing: In a bowl whisk together oil, lime juice, honey, mustard, cumin, garlic, salt and pepper. Just before serving, drizzle over salad and toss gently.

Per serving (8)	
Calories	119
Protein	2 g
Carbohydrates	14 g
Dietary Fiber	3 g
Fat - Total	7 g
Saturated Fat	1 g
Calcium	51 mg

Basil, Potato and Green Bean Salad

SERVES 6 TO 8

A simple way to trim fat in salad dressings is to replace part of the oil called for in the recipe with chicken or vegetable stock. That's what I do here in this light, appealing summer salad.

TIP

This pesto-style dressing is also great with other vegetable and pasta salads. Make it ahead and store in a covered container in the refrigerator for 1 week.

VARIATION

Tuna, Potato and Bean Salad

Add 1 can (6 1/2 oz [184 g]) solid white tuna, drained and flaked for a meal-in-one salad supper.

2 lbs	small new potatoes, cut into chunks	1 kg
1 lb	green beans, trimmed and cut into 2-inch (5 cm) pieces	500 g
1	small red onion, thinly sliced	1

Dressing

1/2 cup	packed fresh basil	125 mL
1/3 cup	chicken stock *or* vegetable stock	75 mL
1/4 cup	olive oil	50 mL
1/4 cup	white wine vinegar	50 mL
2 tbsp	Dijon mustard	25 mL
1 tbsp	balsamic vinegar	15 mL
2	cloves garlic	2
1/2 tsp	salt	2 mL
1/2 tsp	pepper	2 mL

1. Cook potatoes in a large saucepan of boiling salted water for 10 minutes or until tender. Remove with slotted spoon to a salad bowl. Add beans to saucepan and bring to a boil; cook 3 to 5 minutes or until tender-crisp. Drain and chill under cold water; drain again. Add beans and onion to salad bowl.

2. Dressing: In a food processor or blender, purée basil, stock, oil, wine vinegar, mustard, balsamic vinegar, garlic, salt and pepper. Pour over potato mixture; toss well. Cover and refrigerate if making ahead; serve within 4 hours.

Per serving (8)	
Calories	176
Protein	4 g
Carbohydrates	26 g
Dietary Fiber	4 g
Fat - Total	7 g
Saturated Fat	1 g
Calcium	42 mg

Speedy Mexicali Rice and Black Bean Salad

Your turn to bring the salad to the next reunion or neighborhood get-together? Here's a sure-fire crowd pleaser which can be easily doubled to feed as many folks as the occasion demands. Even better, it can be made a day ahead.

TIP

To cook the rice, rinse 3/4 cup (175 mL) basmati rice under cold water; drain. In a medium saucepan, bring 1 1/2 cups (375 mL) water to a boil. Add rice and 1/2 tsp (2 mL) salt; cover and simmer for 15 minutes or until tender. Spread hot rice on baking sheet to cool.

Salad

2 cups	cooked basmati rice	500 mL
1	can (19 oz [540 mL]) black beans, rinsed and drained	1
1 cup	cooked corn kernels	250 mL
1	red bell pepper, diced	1
4	green onions, chopped	4

Dressing

1/2 cup	light sour cream	125 mL
2 tbsp	olive oil	25 mL
4 tsp	freshly squeezed lime juice *or* lemon juice	20 mL
1 tsp	dried oregano	5 mL
1 tsp	ground cumin	5 mL
1/2 tsp	hot pepper sauce	2 mL
1/2 cup	chopped fresh coriander *or* parsley	125 mL

1. Salad: In a large serving bowl, combine rice, black beans, corn, red pepper and green onions.
2. Dressing: In a bowl, combine sour cream, olive oil, lime juice, oregano, cumin and hot pepper sauce. Pour over rice mixture; toss well. Cover and refrigerate for up to 8 hours. Stir in coriander just before serving.

Per serving	
Calories	202
Protein	7 g
Carbohydrates	32 g
Dietary Fiber	5 g
Fat - Total	6 g
Saturated Fat	1.6 g
Calcium	54 mg

When preparing this dish ahead, I like to keep the blanched green beans, tomatoes and dressing separate and toss them just before serving to prevent the salad from getting soggy.

TIP

Use the terrific mustardy dressing with other favorite vegetable salad mixtures and crisp greens.

Per serving	
Calories	129
Protein	2 g
Carbohydrates	11 g
Dietary Fiber	4 g
Fat - Total	10 g
Saturated Fat	1.3 g
Calcium	42 mg

Green Bean and Plum Tomato Salad

Dressing

1/4 cup	olive oil	50 mL
4 tsp	red wine vinegar	20 mL
1 tbsp	grainy mustard	15 mL
1	clove garlic, minced	1
1/2 tsp	granulated sugar	2 mL
1/4 tsp	salt	1 mL
1/4 tsp	pepper	1 mL
1/4 cup	chopped parsley	50 mL

Salad

1 lb	young green beans, trimmed	500 g
8	small plum tomatoes (about 1 lb [500 g])	8
2	green onions, chopped	2

1. Dressing: In a small bowl, whisk together oil, vinegar, mustard, garlic, sugar, salt and pepper. Stir in parsley.

2. Salad: Cook beans in a medium saucepan of boiling salted water for 3 to 5 minutes or until just tender-crisp. Drain and rinse under cold water to chill; drain well. Pat dry with paper towels or wrap in a clean, dry towel. Cut plum tomatoes in half lengthwise; using a small spoon, scoop out centers. Cut each piece again in half lengthwise; place in a bowl.

3. Just before serving, combine beans, tomatoes and green onions in a serving bowl. Pour dressing over and toss well.

Here, I've borrowed ingredients from the popular Caesar salad dressing to give new potatoes a tasty twist. If you like, cook or microwave 4 bacon strips until crisp, then crumble and sprinkle over salad along with the parsley.

TIP

Refrigerate the salad if making ahead, but let it come to room temperature before serving. Instead of anchovy paste, use 2 minced anchovy fillets. Use potatoes the same size so they cook evenly.

Caesar Potato Salad

2 lbs	small new potatoes (about 18 to 20), scrubbed	1 kg
1/4 cup	light mayonnaise	50 mL
2 tbsp	olive oil	25 mL
2 tbsp	freshly squeezed lemon juice	25 mL
2 tsp	Dijon mustard	10 mL
1 1/2 tsp	anchovy paste	7 mL
1 tsp	Worcestershire sauce	5 mL
1	large clove garlic, minced	1
	Salt and pepper	
	Romaine lettuce	
2 tbsp	chopped parsley	25 mL

1. Cook potatoes in a large saucepan of boiling salted water for 15 minutes or until just tender when pierced. Drain; let cool slightly. Cut into halves or quarters. Place in a bowl.

2. In a small bowl, whisk together mayonnaise, oil, lemon juice, mustard, anchovy paste, Worcestershire sauce and garlic; season with salt and pepper to taste. Pour over warm potatoes; gently toss to coat. Cover and refrigerate up to 4 hours. Arrange in a lettuce-lined serving bowl; sprinkle with parsley.

Per serving	
Calories	192
Protein	3 g
Carbohydrates	28 g
Dietary Fiber	2 g
Fat - Total	8 g
Saturated Fat	1.3 g
Calcium	19 mg

Cut preparation time way down by using store-bought tzatziki in this salad. The garlicky Greek sauce made with yogurt and cucumber is not only great for souvlaki, but also makes a delicious salad dressing to use instead of mayonnaise.

TIP

The salad can be made a day ahead and refrigerated, but I find the flavor is best when served at room temperature.

To seed tomatoes, cut in half crosswise and gently squeeze out seeds.

Great Greek Pasta Salad

8 oz	penne *or* spiral pasta	250 g
1	small red onion, chopped	1
2	bell peppers (assorted colors), diced	2
3/4 cup	crumbled feta cheese	175 mL
1/2 cup	Kalamata olives	125 mL
1/4 cup	chopped parsley	50 mL

Dressing

3/4 cup	TZATZIKI SAUCE (see recipe, page 146)	175 mL
2 tbsp	olive oil	25 mL
1 tbsp	red wine vinegar	15 mL
1 tsp	dried oregano	5 mL
1/4 tsp	pepper	1 mL

1. Cook pasta in a large pot of boiling salted water until tender but firm. Drain; rinse under cold water to chill. Drain well. In a serving bowl, combine pasta, onion, bell peppers, feta, olives and parsley.

2. Dressing: In a bowl combine TZATZIKI SAUCE, oil, vinegar, oregano and pepper; toss with pasta mixture to coat. Cover and refrigerate. Remove from fridge 30 minutes before serving.

Per serving	
Calories	258
Protein	9 g
Carbohydrates	32 g
Dietary Fiber	2 g
Fat - Total	10 g
Saturated Fat	3.7 g
Calcium	165 mg

Tzatziki Sauce

Most supermarkets now stock this sauce in the dairy section, but here's how to make it at home.

TIP

Sauce can be stored in a covered container in refrigerator for up to 5 days.

3 cups	plain low-fat yogurt	750 mL
1 cup	finely chopped unpeeled cucumber	250 mL
1 tsp	salt	5 mL
2	cloves garlic, minced	2
2 tsp	freshly squeezed lemon juice *or* red wine vinegar	10 mL

1. Place yogurt in a coffee-filter or double paper towel-lined sieve set over a bowl; cover and let drain in the refrigerator for 4 hours or until reduced to 1 1/2 cups (375 mL).

2. In a bowl, sprinkle cucumber with salt. Let stand 20 minutes. Drain in a sieve; squeeze out excess moisture and pat dry with paper towels. In a bowl, combine yogurt, cucumber, garlic and lemon juice.

Per tbsp (15 mL)	
Calories	9
Protein	1 g
Carbohydrates	1 g
Dietary Fiber	0 g
Fat - Total	0 g
Saturated Fat	0 g
Calcium	22 mg

Warm Bacon Cabbage Slaw

You'll find that kids love this stir-fry version of a cabbage salad — and so will you. It's a great way to appreciate this nutritious and economical vegetable.

TIP

Buy a convenient bag of shredded cabbage at your supermarket and this salad is made in no time.

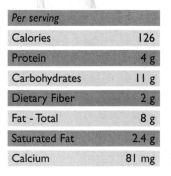

1/4 cup	light sour cream *or* plain yogurt	50 mL
2 tbsp	light mayonnaise	25 mL
2 tbsp	cider vinegar	25 mL
1 tbsp	Dijon mustard	15 mL
1 tbsp	brown sugar	15 mL
3	slices bacon, chopped	3
4 cups	shredded green cabbage	1 L
2	stalks celery, sliced	2
3	green onions, chopped	3
	Salt and pepper	

1. In a small bowl, whisk together sour cream, mayonnaise, vinegar, mustard and brown sugar.

2. In large nonstick skillet over medium-high heat, cook bacon, stirring, for 3 minutes or until crisp. Transfer to paper towels to drain. Pour off all but 2 tsp (10 mL) of fat in skillet. Add cabbage, celery and green onions; cook, stirring, for 2 to 3 minutes or until cabbage is wilted.

3. Remove from heat; stir in sour cream mixture. Sprinkle with bacon; season with salt and pepper to taste. Serve immediately.

Per serving	
Calories	126
Protein	4 g
Carbohydrates	11 g
Dietary Fiber	2 g
Fat - Total	8 g
Saturated Fat	2.4 g
Calcium	81 mg

With the shortcut microwave method, you'll also find this versatile dish a breeze to make for quick family suppers.

TIP

Another option is to cook the potatoes half in the microwave and half in the oven. Cover the potatoes with microwave-safe plastic wrap and microwave at High for 8 minutes; sprinkle with Parmesan and parsley. Finish by baking in a 375° F (190° C) oven for about 25 minutes or until potatoes are tender.

Easy Parmesan Potato Bake

PREHEAT OVEN TO 375° F (190° C)
11- BY 9-INCH (2.5 L) BAKING DISH, BUTTERED

6	medium potatoes, peeled, thinly sliced (about 2 lbs [1 kg])	6
1 cup	chicken stock *or* vegetable stock	250 mL
1 tbsp	melted butter or olive oil	15 mL
1	large clove garlic, minced	1
1/4 tsp	salt	1 mL
1/4 tsp	pepper	1 mL
1/3 cup	grated Parmesan cheese	75 mL
1 tbsp	chopped parsley	15 mL

1. Layer potatoes in prepared baking dish. In a large glass measuring cup, combine stock, butter, garlic, salt and pepper; pour over potatoes. Sprinkle with Parmesan and parsley.
2. Bake in oven for 45 to 55 minutes or until potatoes are tender and top is golden brown.

QUICK MICROWAVE-BROILER METHOD

PREHEAT BROILER

Layer potatoes in baking dish; pour stock mixture over. Cover with lid or microwave-safe plastic wrap; turn back one corner to vent. Microwave at High for 8 minutes. Rearrange potatoes slices. Cover and microwave at High for another 6 to 8 minutes or until potatoes are tender when pierced with a fork. Sprinkle with Parmesan and parsley. Place under broiler, about 5 inches (12 cm) from heat; cook for 2 to 3 minutes or until nicely browned.

Per serving	
Calories	153
Protein	5 g
Carbohydrates	25 g
Dietary Fiber	2 g
Fat - Total	4 g
Saturated Fat	2.4 g
Calcium	86 mg

SERVES 4 TO 6

This classic comfort food, called *kugel*, is a staple in Jewish cooking. It's a delicious accompaniment to roasted meats and chicken.

TIP

Wrapping the grated potatoes in a clean dry towel gets rid of excess starch. Make sure to grate potatoes just before using since they discolor quickly.

Potato Pudding

SERVES 4 TO 6

PREHEAT OVEN TO 350° F (180° C)
8-INCH (2 L) SQUARE BAKING DISH, WELL OILED

2	large eggs	2
2 tbsp	all-purpose flour	25 mL
1 tbsp	chopped parsley	15 mL
1	large clove garlic, minced	1
3/4 tsp	salt	4 mL
1/4 tsp	pepper	1 mL
1	medium onion	1
6	medium potatoes (about 2 lbs [1 kg])	6
1 tbsp	vegetable oil	15 mL

1. In a bowl, beat eggs; stir in flour, parsley, garlic, salt and pepper. Using a food processor, grate onion; fold into egg mixture.

2. Peel potatoes; wash and cut into quarters. Grate using a food processor. Wrap in a large clean kitchen towel; squeeze out excess moisture. Stir into onion mixture until combined. (Do this quickly before potatoes discolor.)

3. Spread in baking dish. Drizzle with oil and spread evenly. Bake in oven for about 1 hour or until top is nicely browned. Cut into squares and serve.

Per serving (6)	
Calories	166
Protein	5 g
Carbohydrates	28 g
Dietary Fiber	2 g
Fat - Total	4 g
Saturated Fat	0.7 g
Calcium	20 mg

SERVES 4

If you're like me, you'll come to rely on this breezy side dish as the perfect complement to a Sunday roast. I also like it with QUICK BISTRO-STYLE STEAK (see recipe, page 105) and other grilled meats.

TIP

Peel the potatoes if you like, but I find the potatoes are tastier with the skin left on.

Roasted Garlic Potatoes

PREHEAT OVEN TO 400° F (200° C)
13- BY 9-INCH (3 L) BAKING DISH, OILED

4	baking potatoes (about 2 1/4 lbs [1.125 kg]), scrubbed and cut into 1-inch (2.5 cm) chunks	4
2 tbsp	olive oil	25 mL
4	cloves garlic, slivered	4
	Salt and pepper	
1 tbsp	chopped parsley	15 mL

1. Cook potato chunks in a large saucepan of boiling salted water for 5 minutes; drain well. Spread in baking dish. Drizzle with oil and garlic; season with salt and pepper to taste.

2. Roast for 40 minutes, stirring occasionally, until potatoes are tender and golden. Sprinkle with parsley.

Per serving	
Calories	290
Protein	5 g
Carbohydrates	53 g
Dietary Fiber	5 g
Fat - Total	7 g
Saturated Fat	1 g
Calcium	27 mg

Easy Skillet Corn with Tomatoes and Basil

Fresh corn is a real summer treat. Serve this tasty summer side dish with grilled meats.

TIP

Fresh corn works best, but frozen niblets can be substituted. To cut corn kernels from cobs, stand ears on end and cut straight down using a small sharp knife.

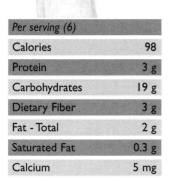

2 tsp	vegetable oil or olive oil	10 mL
3	green onions, chopped	3
1	small green bell pepper, diced	1
3 cups	uncooked corn kernels (about 5 ears of corn)	750 mL
2	tomatoes, seeded and diced	2
2 tbsp	chopped fresh basil (or 1 tsp [5 mL] dried)	25 mL
Pinch	granulated sugar	Pinch
	Salt and pepper	

1. In a large nonstick skillet, heat oil over medium-high heat. Add green onions, green pepper, corn, tomatoes and basil (if using dried); cook, stirring often, for 5 to 7 minutes (8 to 10 minutes, if using frozen corn) or until corn is tender. Add sugar; season with salt and pepper to taste. Sprinkle with chopped basil (if using fresh).

Per serving (6)	
Calories	98
Protein	3 g
Carbohydrates	19 g
Dietary Fiber	3 g
Fat - Total	2 g
Saturated Fat	0.3 g
Calcium	5 mg

SERVES 4

Roasting brings out the best in many vegetables, including asparagus. The oven-roasting method is much simpler than the traditional way of cooking asparagus in a steamer or pot of boiling water.

TIP

Place sesame seeds on a rimmed baking sheet; toast in oven while roasting asparagus for 4 to 5 minutes or until lightly colored. Transfer to a bowl; let cool.

Oven-Roasted Sesame Asparagus

PREHEAT OVEN TO 400° F (200° C)
13- BY 9-INCH (3 L) BAKING DISH

1 lb	asparagus	500 g
1 tbsp	olive oil	15 mL
1 tbsp	soya sauce	15 mL
2 tsp	balsamic vinegar	10 mL
1 tbsp	toasted sesame seeds (see Tip, at left)	15 mL
1/2 tsp	toasted sesame oil (optional)	2 mL

1. Snap off tough asparagus ends and, if large, peel stalks. Arrange in a single layer in baking dish. Drizzle with oil; roast in oven, stirring occasionally, for 15 minutes.

2. In a bowl combine soya sauce and balsamic vinegar; drizzle over asparagus. Roast 5 minutes more or until tender-crisp. Remove from oven; sprinkle with sesame seeds and sesame oil, if using.

Per serving	
Calories	71
Protein	4 g
Carbohydrates	6 g
Dietary Fiber	1 g
Fat - Total	5 g
Saturated Fat	0.6 g
Calcium	29 mg

SERVES 4

Teriyaki Vegetable Stir-Fry

Use this recipe as a guideline and then get creative with whatever vegetables you have in the fridge. You'll need about 5 cups (1.25 L) in total.

TIP

Vegetables that take longer to cook – such as carrots, broccoli and cauliflower – should be added to the skillet first before adding quick-cooking ones like peppers and zucchini.

You can also toss the cooked vegetables with 4 oz (125 g) cooked spaghettini for any easy pasta supper.

2 tbsp	teriyaki sauce *or* soya sauce	25 mL
1 tbsp	rice vinegar	15 mL
2 tsp	brown sugar	10 mL
1 tsp	cornstarch	5 mL
1	large clove garlic, minced	1
1 tbsp	vegetable oil	15 mL
2 cups	small cauliflower florets *or* broccoli florets	500 mL
1	red bell pepper, cut into 2-inch (5 cm) strips	1
2	small zucchini, halved lengthwise and thinly sliced	2

1. In a glass measuring cup, combine teriyaki sauce with 2 tbsp (25 mL) water. Stir in vinegar, brown sugar, cornstarch and garlic; set aside.

2. In a wok or large nonstick skillet, heat oil over high heat. Add cauliflower and cook, stirring, for 1 minute. Add red pepper and zucchini; cook, stirring, for 2 minutes. Reduce heat to medium. Add teriyaki sauce mixture; cook, stirring, until sauce is slightly thickened. Cover and cook for 1 minute or until vegetables are tender-crisp.

Per serving	
Calories	76
Protein	2 g
Carbohydrates	10 g
Dietary Fiber	2 g
Fat - Total	4 g
Saturated Fat	0.3 g
Calcium	23 mg

This hearty vegetable dish is reminiscent of Swiss cheese fondue. It can even stand in for a light, satisfying supper when-paired with crusty bread and a tossed salad.

TIP

Nutmeg is a key flavoring in this dish. Whole nutmeg is preferable to the pre-ground variety. Find it in the spice section of supermarkets and use a special grater available in kitchenware shops.

Cauliflower Fondue Bake

PREHEAT OVEN TO 375° F (190° C)
8-INCH (2 L) SQUARE BAKING DISH, BUTTERED

1	medium cauliflower, broken into florets	1
2 tbsp	butter	25 mL
2 tbsp	all-purpose flour	25 mL
1/2 cup	milk	125 mL
1/2 cup	dry white wine	125 mL
1 1/2 cups	shredded Swiss Gruyere cheese	375 mL
	Salt and freshly grated nutmeg	

1. Cook cauliflower in a large saucepan of boiling salted water for 3 minutes or until tender-crisp. Drain well; place in baking dish.

2. In the same saucepan, melt butter over medium heat; blend in flour and cook, stirring, for 15 seconds or until bubbly. Whisk in milk in a stream; cook until smooth and very thick. Whisk in wine in a stream; cook, stirring, until thickened and bubbly. Reduce heat to low; gradually add cheese, a handful at a time, stirring, until cheese melts and sauce is smooth. Season with salt and generous pinch of nutmeg to taste. Sauce will be thick.

3. Pour evenly over cauliflower. (The dish can be prepared to this point up to a day ahead; cover and refrigerate.) Bake for 20 to 25 minutes (up to 10 minutes longer, if refrigerated) or until cauliflower is just tender and top is lightly browned.

Per serving	
Calories	197
Protein	11 g
Carbohydrates	7 g
Dietary Fiber	2 g
Fat - Total	13 g
Saturated Fat	7.8 g
Calcium	317 mg

I love the combination of sweet potatoes and apples accented with maple syrup. It's great served with pork or chicken.

TIP

Use 2 lbs (1 kg) butternut squash, peeled and seeds removed, instead of sweet potatoes.

You can make this vegetable dish a day ahead; cover and refrigerate. To reheat, cover and microwave at High until piping hot.

Microwave Sweet Potato Purée with Apples

8-CUP (2 L) CASSEROLE DISH

1 tbsp	butter	15 mL
1	small onion, chopped	1
2 lbs	sweet potatoes, (about 3) peeled and cut into 1 1/2-inch (4 cm) chunks	1 kg
2	apples, peeled, cored and chopped	2
1/4 cup	maple syrup	50 mL
	Salt, pepper and nutmeg	

1. In casserole dish, combine butter and onion; microwave at High for 2 minutes or until onion is softened. Add sweet potatoes and apples; drizzle with maple syrup. Cover and microwave at High for 20 to 25 minutes, stirring once, until sweet potatoes are very tender.

2. In a food processor, purée in batches until smooth. Place in a serving dish; season with salt, pepper and nutmeg to taste.

Per serving (6)	
Calories	183
Protein	2 g
Carbohydrates	41 g
Dietary Fiber	4 g
Fat - Total	2 g
Saturated Fat	1.3 g
Calcium	41 mg

SERVES 4

A favorite do-ahead vegetable dish for holiday dinners, this can be prepared a day in advance and quickly reheated in the microwave.

TIP

A combination of thin strips of carrots and rutabaga can be prepared in the same way.

Balsamic-Glazed Carrots

1 lb	peeled baby carrots	500 g
1 tbsp	butter	15 mL
4 tsp	balsamic vinegar *or* red wine vinegar	20 mL
	Salt, pepper and granulated sugar	

1. In a medium saucepan of boiling lightly salted water, cook carrots for 5 to 7 minutes or until tender-crisp; drain well. Return to saucepan.

2. Add butter and vinegar; season with salt, pepper and a pinch of sugar to taste. Cook over medium heat, stirring, for 2 minutes or until liquid has evaporated and carrots are lightly glazed.

Per serving	
Calories	78
Protein	1 g
Carbohydrates	12 g
Dietary Fiber	4 g
Fat - Total	3 g
Saturated Fat	1.8 g
Calcium	34 mg

CAKES, COOKIES & DESSERTS

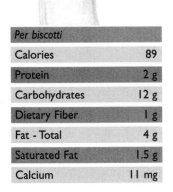

MAKES ABOUT 4 DOZEN COOKIES

Crunchy Almond Biscotti

PREHEAT OVEN TO 325° F (160° C)
BAKING SHEETS, GREASED

Biscotti are all the rage these days. And why not? They are much easier to bake than delicate cookies like shortbread and they're also lower in fat.

TIP

Keep cookies stored in a covered container, separating layers with waxed paper, for up to 1 week, or freeze for up to 1 month. These cookies travel well and are perfect for mailing to special friends.

1/2 cup	butter, softened	125 mL
1 1/4 cups	granulated sugar	300 mL
3	large eggs	3
1 tbsp	grated lemon zest	15 mL
1 tsp	almond extract	5 mL
3 cups	all-purpose flour	750 mL
2 1/2 tsp	baking powder	12 mL
1/2 tsp	salt	2 mL
1 cup	whole unblanched almonds, coarsely chopped	250 mL

1. In a bowl using an electric mixer, cream butter with sugar until fluffy. Beat in eggs, one at a time, until incorporated; beat in lemon zest and almond extract. In another bowl, combine flour, baking powder and salt; stir into butter mixture until combined. Stir in chopped almonds.

2. Turn out dough onto a lightly floured surface. With floured hands, shape into a ball; divide dough in half. Shape each piece into a log about 14 inches (35 cm) long. Place 3 inches (8 cm) apart on sheet; flatten to 2 inches (5 cm) in width, with slightly rounded top.

3. Bake for 25 to 30 minutes or until lightly colored and firm to the touch. Let cool on baking sheets for 10 minutes. With long spatula, transfer to a cutting board. With a large serrated knife, cut on a slight diagonal into 1/2-inch (1 cm) slices. Arrange slices upright, 1 inch (2.5 cm) apart on baking sheet. (Use 2 sheets if necessary.)

4. Bake for 15 to 20 minutes or until dry and lightly browned. Let cool on rack.

Per biscotti	
Calories	89
Protein	2 g
Carbohydrates	12 g
Dietary Fiber	1 g
Fat - Total	4 g
Saturated Fat	1.5 g
Calcium	11 mg

MAKES 24 BARS

Making these bars is a lot less work than making a batch of cookies. Save even more time by using a food processor to make the shortcrust base.

TIP

For easy slicing, line pan with greased foil. Once baked, place pan of bars in freezer for 30 minutes or until firm; lift out and cut into bars using a sharp-tipped knife. Arrange in covered container, separating layers with waxed paper and refrigerate. Or, freeze for up to 1 month.

Per bar	
Calories	115
Protein	1 g
Carbohydrates	17 g
Dietary Fiber	1 g
Fat - Total	5 g
Saturated Fat	2 g
Calcium	14 mg

Easy Apricot Pecan Bars

PREHEAT OVEN TO 350° F (180° C)
8-INCH (2 L) SQUARE BAKING PAN,
LINED WITH FOIL AND GREASED

Base

1 cup	all-purpose flour	250 mL
6 tbsp	butter, cut into pieces	90 mL
1/4 cup	packed brown sugar	50 mL

Topping

1 cup	dried apricots	250 mL
1	large egg	1
1 tsp	vanilla	5 mL
3/4 cup	packed light brown sugar	175 mL
2 tbsp	all-purpose flour	25 mL
1/2 tsp	baking powder	2 mL
1/2 cup	chopped pecans *or* walnuts	125 mL

1. Base: In a food processor, combine flour, butter and brown sugar; process to make fine crumbs. Press mixture evenly in bottom of prepared baking pan. Bake for 15 minutes or until light golden. Let cool; leave oven on.

2. Topping: Place apricots in a small saucepan; cover with water. Bring to a boil; cook for 3 to 5 minutes or until softened. Drain well; let cool slightly. Using scissors, cut into slivers.

3. In a bowl, beat egg with vanilla; stir in brown sugar, flour and baking powder. Add apricots. Spread mixture evenly over baked crust; sprinkle with pecans. Bake for 22 to 25 minutes or until top is golden brown. Place on rack; let cool.

MAKES 24 BARS

Ideal for school lunches, these chewy bars travel well. I like to package bars individually in plastic wrap, place in a covered container and freeze. It's so easy to pop a bar from the freezer into lunchbags or take them along for snacks.

TIP

Lining the baking pan with foil makes it a breeze to remove bars and ensures a fast clean-up.

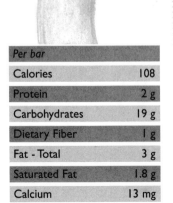

Lunch-Box Oatmeal Raisin Bars

PREHEAT OVEN TO 350° F (180° C)
13- BY 9-INCH (3.5 L) BAKING PAN LINED WITH FOIL, GREASED

2/3 cup	packed brown sugar	150 mL
1/3 cup	butter *or* margarine	75 mL
1/3 cup	golden corn syrup	75 mL
2 1/2 cups	rolled oats	625 mL
1/4 cup	all-purpose flour	50 mL
1/2 cup	raisins *or* chopped dried apricots	125 mL
1	large egg	1
1 tsp	vanilla	5 mL

1. In a glass bowl, combine brown sugar, butter and corn syrup. Microwave at High for 2 minutes; stir until smooth. Microwave 1 minute more or until sugar dissolves and mixture comes to a full boil.

2. Stir in rolled oats, flour and raisins. In a small bowl, beat egg with vanilla. Stir into rolled-oats mixture.

3. Spread evenly in prepared pan. Bake for 20 to 25 minutes or until golden around edges. Let cool 10 minutes in pan. Lift out foil; cut into 3- by 1 1/2-inch (8 by 4 cm) bars. Transfer to a rack to complete cooling.

Per bar	
Calories	108
Protein	2 g
Carbohydrates	19 g
Dietary Fiber	1 g
Fat - Total	3 g
Saturated Fat	1.8 g
Calcium	13 mg

GREEN BEAN AND PLUM TOMATO SALAD (PAGE 143)

Zucchini gives this cake a rich, moist texture. There's no visible trace of it when the cake is baked, so it's perfect to serve to reluctant zucchini eaters. I don't bother to peel the zucchini, but you can if you prefer. Shredding the zucchini in a food processor saves time.

TIP

If you don't have a flour sifter, sift the dry ingredients through a fine-meshed sieve to remove any lumps. The chocolate glaze is optional; instead, you can sift icing sugar over cake just before serving.

Double Chocolate Snacking Cake

PREHEAT OVEN TO 350° F (180° C)
13- BY 9-INCH (3.5 L) CAKE PAN, GREASED

2	large eggs	2
1 cup	light sour cream *or* plain yogurt	250 mL
1/2 cup	vegetable oil	125 mL
2 tsp	vanilla	10 mL
2 cups	finely shredded zucchini	500 mL
2 1/4 cups	all-purpose flour	550 mL
1 1/3 cups	granulated sugar	325 mL
1/2 cup	cocoa powder	125 mL
1 tsp	baking powder	5 mL
1 tsp	baking soda	5 mL
1/2 tsp	salt	2 mL
3/4 cup	semi-sweet chocolate chips	175 mL
3/4 cup	chopped walnuts	175 mL
	CHOCOLATE GLAZE (optional) (recipe follows)	

1. In a large bowl, beat eggs; beat in sour cream, oil and vanilla. Stir in shredded zucchini.

2. In another bowl, sift together flour, sugar, cocoa, baking powder, baking soda and salt. Stir into creamed mixture until just combined. Fold in chocolate chips and walnuts.

3. Spread batter evenly in pan. Bake for 45 to 50 minutes or until a cake tester inserted in center comes out clean. Let stand on rack for 15 minutes to cool. Spread glaze over warm cake; let cool completely.

Chocolate Glaze

1 cup	icing sugar	250 mL
2 tbsp	cocoa powder	25 mL
2 tbsp	milk	25 mL

1. In a bowl combine icing sugar, cocoa powder and milk; stir to make a smooth, spreadable glaze.

Per serving (with glaze)	
Calories	267
Protein	5 g
Carbohydrates	38 g
Dietary Fiber	2 g
Fat - Total	12 g
Saturated Fat	3 g
Calcium	34 mg

≺ LEMON FOOL WITH FRESH BERRIES (PAGE 172)

Here's a lemony-flavored loaf that stays moist for days — if it lasts that long.

TIP

I like to double this recipe so that I have an extra loaf handy in the freezer. Wrap in plastic wrap, then in foil and freeze for up to 1 month.

VARIATION

Lemon Poppy Seed Loaf
Stir 2 tbsp (25 mL) poppy seeds into flour mixture before combining with yogurt mixture.

Lemon Yogurt Loaf

**PREHEAT OVEN TO 350° F (180° C)
9- BY 5-INCH (2 L) LOAF PAN, GREASED**

1 3/4 cups	all-purpose flour	425 mL
1 tsp	baking powder	5 mL
1/2 tsp	baking soda	2 mL
1/4 tsp	salt	1 mL
2	large eggs	2
3/4 cup	granulated sugar	175 mL
3/4 cup	plain low-fat yogurt	175 mL
1/3 cup	vegetable oil	75 mL
1 tbsp	grated lemon zest	15 mL

Topping

1/3 cup	freshly squeezed lemon juice	75 mL
1/3 cup	granulated sugar	75 mL

1. In a bowl combine flour, baking powder, baking soda and salt. In another large bowl, beat eggs; stir in sugar, yogurt, oil and lemon zest. Fold in flour mixture to make a smooth batter.

2. Spoon into prepared pan; bake for 50 to 60 minutes or until cake tester inserted in center comes out clean. Place pan on rack.

3. Topping: In a small saucepan, heat lemon juice and sugar; bring to a boil. Cook, stirring, until sugar is dissolved. (Or place in a glass bowl and microwave at High for 1 minute, stirring once.) Pour over hot loaf in pan; let cool completely before turning out of pan.

Per slice	
Calories	161
Protein	3 g
Carbohydrates	25 g
Dietary Fiber	0 g
Fat - Total	6 g
Saturated Fat	0.7 g
Calcium	27 mg

SERVES 12

This crowd-pleasing cake is as easy to make as a batch of muffins. Serve it as a dessert or enjoy it with a fresh-brewed cup of coffee or tea.

TIP

To freeze, wrap in plastic wrap, then in foil. Cake freezes well for up to 1 month.

Per serving	
Calories	299
Protein	5 g
Carbohydrates	47 g
Dietary Fiber	1 g
Fat - Total	10 g
Saturated Fat	6.1 g
Calcium	48 mg

Blueberry Crumb Cake

PREHEAT OVEN TO 350° F (180° C)
9-INCH (23 CM) SPRINGFORM PAN, GREASED

Crumb topping

1/2 cup	all-purpose flour	125 mL
1/3 cup	packed brown sugar	75 mL
1 tsp	cinnamon	5 mL
1/4 cup	butter, cut into pieces	50 mL

Cake

2 cups	all-purpose flour	500 mL
1 cup	granulated sugar	250 mL
2 1/2 tsp	baking powder	12 mL
1/2 tsp	baking soda	2 mL
1/2 tsp	salt	2 mL
2 cups	fresh or frozen blueberries	500 mL
2	large eggs	2
3/4 cup	plain low-fat yogurt	175 mL
1/3 cup	butter, melted and cooled	75 mL
1 1/2 tsp	grated lemon zest	7 mL

1. Crumb topping: In a bowl, combine flour, brown sugar and cinnamon. Using a pastry blender or your fingertips, blend in butter until crumbly.

2. Cake: In a large mixing bowl, stir together flour, sugar, baking powder, soda and salt. Toss blueberries with 2 tbsp (25 mL) of the flour mixture; set aside.

3. In another bowl, beat eggs; beat in yogurt, melted butter and lemon zest. Stir in flour mixture to make a smooth batter. Gently fold in floured blueberries. (Batter will be thick.)

4. Spoon into prepared pan. Sprinkle top with crumb mixture. Bake in oven for 50 to 60 minutes or until cake tester inserted in center comes out clean. Let cool on rack. Run a knife around edge; remove side of pan, remove base and transfer cake to serving plate.

Luscious Tropical Cheesecake

Making a cheesecake may seem like a half-day production, but not with this no-bake method that is guaranteed to win raves for the cook.

TIP

Can be made the day ahead, cover and refrigerate.

To toast coconut, place on baking sheet in a 350° F (180° C) oven, stirring once, for 5 to 6 minutes.

PREHEAT OVEN TO 350° F (180° C)
9-INCH (2 L) SPRINGFORM PAN

Crust

1 cup	digestive cookie crumbs *or* graham wafer crumbs	250 mL
2 tbsp	granulated sugar	25 mL
2 tbsp	butter, melted	25 mL

Filling

1	can (14 oz [398 mL]) crushed pineapple	1
1	pkg (1/4 oz [7 g]) unflavored gelatin	1
1	pkg (8 oz [250 g]) light cream cheese, softened and cubed	1
1 cup	low-fat ricotta cheese	250 mL
1/2 cup	granulated sugar	125 mL
1 1/2 tsp	grated orange zest	7 mL
1 cup	whipping (35%) cream	250 mL
1/2 cup	sweetened desiccated coconut, toasted	125 mL

1. Crust: In a bowl combine cookie crumbs, sugar and butter. Press in bottom of springform pan. Bake for 8 minutes or until set. Chill until firm. Fit a 3-inch (8 cm) wide strip of waxed or parchment paper around inside of pan.

2. Filling: Drain pineapple in sieve set over bowl; press with rubber spatula to extract juice. Pour 1/2 cup (125 mL) of the juice into a small saucepan; sprinkle gelatin over. Let stand for 5 minutes to soften. Cook over low heat, stirring, until gelatin is dissolved. (Or put juice and gelatin in a measuring cup; let stand 5 minutes to soften, then microwave at Medium for 1 minute.) Let cool slightly.

3. In a food processor, combine cream cheese, ricotta, sugar and warm gelatin mixture; process until smooth. Transfer to a large bowl; stir in drained pineapple and orange zest.

Per serving (10)	
Calories	295
Protein	7 g
Carbohydrates	25 g
Dietary Fiber	1 g
Fat - Total	19 g
Saturated Fat	12.2 g
Calcium	120 mg

4. In a bowl using an electric mixer, whip cream until stiff peaks form. Fold into pineapple mixture until smooth. Pour into prepared pan; smooth top and sprinkle with toasted coconut. Chill until set, about 4 hours. Remove side of pan and waxed or parchment paper; arrange on a serving plate.

Strawberry Mascarpone Trifle with Chocolate

No cooking is involved in this sensational dessert! It's only a matter of assembling layers of pound cake, luscious strawberries, creamy mascarpone and dark chocolate. Sinful — and oh so simple.

TIP

Instead of the mascarpone cheese, you can use 1 pkg (8 oz [250 g]) light cream cheese.

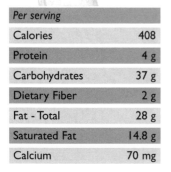

1 cup	mascarpone cheese	250 mL
2/3 cup	granulated sugar	150 mL
2 tbsp	orange juice	25 mL
1 tbsp	grated orange zest	15 mL
1 1/2 cups	whipping (35%) cream	375 mL
5 cups	fresh strawberries	1.25 L
1/3 cup	orange-flavored liqueur *or* orange juice	75 mL
1	frozen pound cake (10 oz [298 g])	1
4	squares bittersweet or semi-sweet chocolate (4 oz [125 g]), grated	4
	Mint sprigs	

1. In a bowl, beat mascarpone cheese with sugar, orange juice and zest until creamy. In another bowl using an electric mixer, beat cream until stiff peaks form; fold into mascarpone mixture until smooth.

2. Set aside 1 cup (250 mL) small whole strawberries. Slice remaining berries and place in a bowl; stir in orange-flavored liqueur.

3. Cut cake into 1- by 1/2-inch (2.5 by 1 cm) pieces. Arrange half the cake cubes in bottom of an 8-cup (2 L) glass serving bowl. Top with half the sliced strawberries, including some liquid. Spread with half the mascarpone mixture; sprinkle with half the grated chocolate. Repeat layers with remaining ingredients.

4. Cover and refrigerate at least 4 hours and up to 12 hours before serving. Garnish with reserved whole strawberries and mint sprigs.

Per serving	
Calories	408
Protein	4 g
Carbohydrates	37 g
Dietary Fiber	2 g
Fat - Total	28 g
Saturated Fat	14.8 g
Calcium	70 mg

Wine-Poached Pear Fans

SERVES 4

When I want elegance and style, I turn to this classic preparation for pears. It's an impressive way to end a special meal.

TIP

Poach the pears a day ahead. They are best served well-chilled.

Select pears that are not overly ripe so they will hold their shape when sliced.

Extra-thick yogurt, a low-fat alternative to sour cream is available in most supermarkets. Or make your own by placing 1 1/2 cups (375 mL) plain yogurt in a sieve lined with a paper coffee filter or double layer of paper towels. Set sieve over a bowl to drain; cover and refrigerate for 3 hours or until yogurt is reduced by half.

2 cups	red wine *or* cranberry juice cocktail	500 mL
1/2 cup	granulated sugar	125 mL
1	cinnamon stick	1
3	whole cloves	3
2	strips orange zest (each 3 inches [8 cm] long)	2
4	Bartlett pears, peeled, halved and cored	4
	Whipped cream *or* extra-thick yogurt	
	Freshly grated nutmeg	
	Mint sprigs	

1. In a medium saucepan, combine wine, sugar, cinnamon stick, cloves and orange zest. Bring to a boil; stir to dissolve sugar. Add pear halves; reduce heat, cover and simmer for 15 minutes or until just tender when pierced with a knife. Remove with a slotted spoon to a dish; let cool.

2. Bring poaching liquid in saucepan to a boil over high heat; boil until reduced to 3/4 cup (175 mL). Strain through a sieve to remove spices; let cool and refrigerate.

3. Place pears cut-side down on work surface. Beginning near the stem end, cut each pear half lengthwise into slices 1/4 inch (5 mm) thick. (Do not cut through the stem itself; slices will still be attached at stem end.) Arrange 2 pear halves on each dessert plate, pressing down gently to fan out slices. Spoon syrup over. Garnish with a dollop of whipped cream and sprinkle with grated nutmeg. Garnish with mint sprigs.

Per serving (without garnish)	
Calories	242
Protein	1 g
Carbohydrates	52 g
Dietary Fiber	5 g
Fat - Total	1 g
Saturated Fat	0 g
Calcium	36 mg

SERVES 6

Fresh Fruit Ginger Compote

Here, candied ginger dresses up a simple homemade or store-bought fruit salad. To further enhance this dessert, add 2 tbsp (25 mL) orange-flavored liqueur. Serve with crisp cookies such as biscotti or lemon snaps.

TIP

Any combination of fruits cut into bite-sized pieces can be used – including pears, peaches, plums, apples, pineapple and strawberries. To prevent discoloration, prepare fruit mixture no more than 4 hours ahead of serving.

1 1/3 cups	orange juice	325 mL
1/4 cup	honey	50 mL
2 tbsp	finely chopped candied ginger	25 mL
2 tsp	grated orange zest	10 mL
6 cups	prepared fresh fruit	1.5 L

1. In a small saucepan, combine orange juice, honey and candied ginger. Bring to a boil; cook for 2 minutes. Remove from heat; stir in orange zest. Let cool to room temperature.

2. Arrange fruit in a serving bowl; pour ginger mixture over. Cover and refrigerate for up to 4 hours before serving.

Per serving	
Calories	159
Protein	1 g
Carbohydrates	41 g
Dietary Fiber	3 g
Fat - Total	1 g
Saturated Fat	0.1 g
Calcium	27 mg

Kids' Favorite Chocolate Pudding

Why rely on expensive store-bought puddings, when you can make nourishing homemade ones that take little time to make on the stovetop or in the microwave? Milk puddings are also a great way to boost calcium.

TIP

Whole milk gives a creamier consistency than low-fat 1% or skim milk in this easy-to-make dessert.

If cooking pudding in the microwave, be sure to use a large bowl to prevent boil-overs.

VARIATION

Butterscotch Pudding
Cook pudding as directed. Substitute 1/2 cup (125 mL) butterscotch chips for the chocolate chips; reduce sugar to 1/4 cup (50 mL).

1/3 cup	granulated sugar	75 mL
1/4 cup	cornstarch	50 mL
2 1/4 cups	milk	550 mL
1/3 cup	semi-sweet chocolate chips	75 mL
1 tsp	vanilla	5 mL

1. In a medium saucepan, whisk together sugar and cornstarch; add milk, whisking until smooth. Place over medium heat; cook, stirring, for 5 minutes or until mixture comes to a full boil; cook for 15 seconds.
2. Remove from heat. Stir in chocolate chips and vanilla; blend until smooth. Pour pudding into individual serving dishes. Let cool slightly; cover surface with plastic wrap to prevent skins from forming on surface. Refrigerate.

MICROWAVE METHOD

In an 8-cup (2 L) glass bowl or casserole dish, whisk together sugar and cornstarch; add milk, whisking until smooth. Microwave at High for 3 minutes. Whisk well; microwave at High for 3 to 4 minutes more, whisking every minute, until pudding comes to a full boil and thickens. Stir in chocolate chips and vanilla.

Per serving	
Calories	233
Protein	5 g
Carbohydrates	40 g
Dietary Fiber	1 g
Fat - Total	7 g
Saturated Fat	4.1 g
Calcium	172 mg

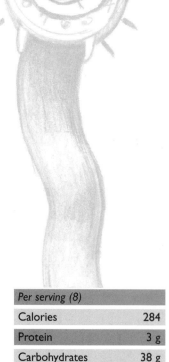

Intimidated by the thought of making two-crust pies? Try this simple free-form pie – it only needs a single pie crust and looks like it came from a pastry shop.

TIP

Store-bought pastry for a single crust pie can be used instead of the suggested homemade pastry.

Per serving (8)	
Calories	284
Protein	3 g
Carbohydrates	38 g
Dietary Fiber	3 g
Fat - Total	15 g
Saturated Fat	7.5 g
Calcium	15 mg

Farmhouse Apple Pie

PREHEAT OVEN TO 375° F (190° C)
LARGE BAKING SHEET, LIGHTLY GREASED

Pastry

1 1/4 cups	all-purpose flour	300 mL
1 tbsp	granulated sugar	15 mL
Pinch	salt	Pinch
1/2 cup	butter, cut into pieces	125 mL
2 tbsp	cold water (approximate)	25 mL

Filling

4	apples, such as Golden Delicious, Spy or Granny Smith, peeled, cored and sliced	4
1/3 cup	granulated sugar	75 mL
1/4 cup	finely chopped pecans	50 mL
1/2 tsp	cinnamon	2 mL

1. Pastry: In a bowl combine flour, sugar and generous pinch of salt. Cut in butter with a pastry blender or use your fingertips to make coarse crumbs. Sprinkle with enough water to hold dough together; gather into a ball. Flatten to a 5-inch (12 cm) circle; wrap in plastic wrap and refrigerate for 30 minutes.

2. On a lightly floured board, roll pastry to a 13-inch (32 cm) circle; transfer to large baking sheet. Using a sharp knife, trim pastry edge to form an even circle.

3. Filling: Starting 2 inches (5 cm) from edge, overlap apple slices in a circle; arrange another overlapping circle of apples in center. In a bowl combine sugar, pecans and cinnamon; sprinkle over apples. Fold pastry rim over apples to form a 2-inch (5 cm) edge.

4. Bake for 35 to 40 minutes or until pastry is golden and apples are tender. Place on rack; let cool. With a spatula, carefully slide pie onto serving platter.

Whip up this batch of muffins and they'll be gone in no time. They are especially child-friendly, but they'll also be enjoyed by the adults in the house.

TIP

Don't overmix the batter. Use quick gentle strokes to combine the dry and liquid ingredients together. It's normal to have a few lumps remaining in the batter.

Banana Spice Muffins

PREHEAT OVEN TO 400° F (200° C)
MUFFIN PAN WITH PAPER LINERS

1	large egg	1
1 cup	mashed ripe bananas (about 3)	250 mL
3/4 cup	packed brown sugar	175 mL
1/2 cup	plain low-fat yogurt	125 mL
1/4 cup	vegetable oil	50 mL
2 cups	all-purpose flour	500 mL
1 1/2 tsp	baking powder	7 mL
1 1/2 tsp	cinnamon	7 mL
1/2 tsp	baking soda	2 mL
1/2 tsp	ground nutmeg	2 mL
1/4 tsp	ground cloves	1 mL
1/4 tsp	salt	1 mL
1/2 cup	raisins	125 mL

1. In a bowl, beat egg; stir in bananas, brown sugar, yogurt and oil until smooth. In another bowl, combine flour, baking powder, cinnamon, baking soda, nutmeg, cloves and salt; stir into banana mixture until just combined. Fold in raisins.

2. Spoon batter into paper-lined muffin cups until level with top of pan. Bake for 20 to 25 minutes or until top springs back when lightly touched. Transfer muffins to a rack and let cool.

Per muffin	
Calories	220
Protein	4 g
Carbohydrates	40 g
Dietary Fiber	2 g
Fat - Total	6 g
Saturated Fat	0.7 g
Calcium	44 mg

Here's an updated version of the traditional "fool" – an old-fashioned dessert with fruit or berries folded into whipped cream or custard. This dessert is ideal for entertaining since it can be assembled earlier in the day.

TIP

Instead of individual serving dishes, layer berries and lemon fool in a 6-cup (1.5 L) deep glass serving bowl.

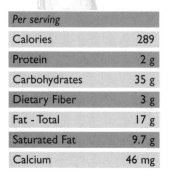

Per serving	
Calories	289
Protein	2 g
Carbohydrates	35 g
Dietary Fiber	3 g
Fat - Total	17 g
Saturated Fat	9.7 g
Calcium	46 mg

Lemon Fool with Fresh Berries

2 tbsp	cornstarch	25 mL
2/3 cup	granulated sugar	150 mL
1 tbsp	grated lemon zest	15 mL
1/3 cup	freshly squeezed lemon juice	75 mL
2	egg yolks	2
1 cup	whipping (35%) cream	250 mL
3 cups	fresh berries, such as sliced strawberries *or* raspberries *or* blueberries	750 mL
	Additional berries, mint sprigs and grated lemon zest	

1. In a small saucepan, combine cornstarch with 1/2 cup (125 mL) cold water; whisk until smooth. Add sugar, lemon zest, juice and egg yolks; cook over medium heat, whisking constantly, until mixture comes to a full boil; cook for 15 seconds. Remove from heat; pour into a large bowl. Let cool slightly. Cover surface with plastic wrap; refrigerate for 2 hours or until chilled. (Recipe can be prepared to this point up to a day ahead.)

2. In a bowl using an electric mixer, whip cream until still peaks form. Whisk lemon mixture until smooth. Whisk in one-quarter of the whipped cream; fold in remaining whipped cream.

3. Arrange half the berries in 6 parfait or large wine glasses. Top with half the lemon fool; layer with remaining berries and lemon fool. (Recipe can be prepared to this point and refrigerated for up to 4 hours.) To serve, garnish with whole berries, mint sprigs and grated lemon zest.

When you pair fresh ripe peaches with a crumbly nut topping, it's a juicy sweet treat. Served warm with ice-cream, it's the ultimate comfort-food dessert.

TIP

Fresh peaches work best, but in a pinch you can substitute 1 can (28 oz [796 mL]) of peaches, drained and sliced. Omit the cornstarch.

Irresistible Peach Almond Crumble

PREHEAT OVEN TO 375° F (190° C)
8-INCH (2 L) BAKING DISH, GREASED

Fruit

4 cups	sliced peeled peaches *or* nectarines	1 L
2 tsp	cornstarch	10 mL
1/3 cup	peach or apricot preserves	75 mL

Topping

1/2 cup	large flake rolled oats	125 mL
1/2 cup	all-purpose flour	125 mL
1/3 cup	packed brown sugar	75 mL
1/3 cup	sliced blanched almonds	75 mL
1/4 tsp	ground ginger	1 mL
1/3 cup	butter, melted	75 mL

1. Fruit: In a bowl toss peaches with cornstarch; stir in preserves. Spread in baking dish.
2. Topping: In a bowl combine rolled oats, flour, brown sugar, almonds and ginger. Pour butter over; stir to make coarse crumbs. Sprinkle over fruit.
3. Bake for 30 to 35 minutes or until topping is golden and filling is bubbly. Serve warm or at room temperature with ice-cream, if desired.

Per serving	
Calories	328
Protein	4 g
Carbohydrates	51 g
Dietary Fiber	4 g
Fat - Total	14 g
Saturated Fat	6.7 g
Calcium	38 mg

SERVES 8

This spectacular tart with a tangy cranberry and marmalade filling is ideal to serve with a steaming cup of fresh-brewed coffee or espresso. Don't let the length of this recipe deter you – it's surprisingly easy to make.

TIP

The baked tart can be wrapped in foil and frozen for 1 month.

Per serving	
Calories	449
Protein	5 g
Carbohydrates	71 g
Dietary Fiber	2 g
Fat - Total	17 g
Saturated Fat	10 g
Calcium	94 mg

Cranberry-Orange Cookie Tart

PREHEAT OVEN TO 350° F (180° C)
10-INCH (25 CM) TART PAN WITH
REMOVABLE BOTTOM, BUTTERED

Filling

2 cups	fresh or frozen cranberries	500 mL
2/3 cup	granulated sugar	150 mL
1/2 cup	orange juice	125 mL
1/2 cup	orange marmalade or raspberry jam	125 mL

Pastry

2 cups	all-purpose flour	500 mL
1/2 cup	granulated sugar	125 mL
1/4 tsp	salt	1 mL
2/3 cup	cold butter, cubed	150 mL
1	egg	1
1 tsp	vanilla	5 mL
1	egg yolk	1
	Icing sugar	

1. Filling: In a medium saucepan, combine cranberries, sugar and orange juice. Bring to a boil; reduce heat and cook, stirring often, for 6 minutes or until thick and jam-like. Stir in marmalade. Remove from heat; let cool.

2. Pastry: In a large bowl, combine flour, sugar and salt. With a pastry blender or fork, cut in butter until mixture resembles fine crumbs. In a small bowl, beat whole egg with vanilla; stir into dry ingredients. Gather dough into a ball and on lightly floured board, knead 3 to 4 times until smooth. Shape dough into 2 discs, one slightly larger than the other. Wrap each in plastic wrap; refrigerate for 1 hour.

3. On a lightly floured surface, roll the larger dough portion into a 12-inch (30 cm) circle. Fit dough into tart pan. Trim edges of pastry, leaving a 1/2-inch (1 cm) overhang. Fold the overhang into the pan and press into pastry to reinforce the sides of the tart. Prick dough in several places with a fork.

4. Spoon cranberry-jam mixture into tart shell. Roll out remaining dough on lightly floured surface into a 10-inch (25 cm) circle. Cut into twelve 3/4-inch (2 cm) strips. Using a long spatula to lift them, arrange 6 strips of dough, spaced about 1/2-inch (1 cm) apart, over jam filling. Arrange remaining strips at right angles to first strips to create a diamond shaped-pattern. Trim edges; press pastry strips against sides of tart to seal. In a small bowl, beat egg yolk with 1 tsp (5 mL) water; brush over pastry strips and edges.

5. Bake for 40 to 45 minutes or until golden. Let cool on rack for 15 minutes. Remove pan rim; let cool completely. Just before serving, sprinkle with icing sugar, if desired.

MAKES 1 1/2 CUPS (375 ML)

Amazing Marshmallow Fudge Sauce

I like to have this versatile, easy-to-make sauce in the fridge for impromptu desserts. It's great poured over ice cream; it's even better when you add sliced bananas or strawberries and a dollop of whipped cream. To create a scrumptious brownie sundae, place a large brownie on a dessert plate, top with a scoop of ice-cream and pour sauce over.

TIP

Keep the sauce in a covered container in the fridge for up to 1 month.

The sauce thickens when refrigerated so, let it come to room temperature before using; it will then pour easily.

1 cup	canned evaporated milk	250 mL
3/4 cup	semi-sweet chocolate chips	175 mL
1 cup	miniature marshmallows	250 mL
1 tsp	vanilla	5 mL

1. Pour evaporated milk in a large glass bowl or casserole dish; microwave at High for 2 to 2 1/2 minutes or until almost boiling. Add chocolate chips; let stand for 2 minutes to melt. Stir well. Add marshmallows; microwave at Medium for 1 1/2 to 2 minutes or until marshmallows are melted. Add vanilla; stir until smooth. Let cool to room temperature before using. Sauce thickens as it cools.

Per tbsp (15 mL)	
Calories	35
Protein	1 g
Carbohydrates	5 g
Dietary Fiber	0 g
Fat - Total	2 g
Saturated Fat	0.9 g
Calcium	27 mg

MAKES 1 1/4 CUPS
(300 ML)

Here's another great sauce for pouring over ice cream. You can also drizzle it over cake, apple pie or fresh fruit.

TIP

Let sauce come to room temperature before using.

Sauce can be stored in a covered container in fridge for up to 1 month.

Quick Butterscotch Sauce

3/4 cup	packed brown sugar	175 mL
3/4 cup	whipping (35%) cream	175 mL
1/4 cup	golden corn syrup	50 mL
1/2 tsp	vanilla	2 mL

1. In a large glass bowl or casserole dish, combine brown sugar, cream and corn syrup. Microwave at High, stirring twice, for 5 to 6 minutes. Add vanilla; let cool to room temperature. Sauce thickens as it cools.

Per tbsp (15 mL)	
Calories	51
Protein	0 g
Carbohydrates	10 g
Dietary Fiber	0 g
Fat - Total	1 g
Saturated Fat	0.9 g
Calcium	9 mg

Maple Custard with Fresh Fruit

Looking for an easy family-pleasing dessert? This one takes only a few minutes to prepare.

TIP

Any kind of fresh, frozen or drained canned fruit can be used. Maple syrup is preferred, but maple-flavored pancake syrup can be substituted.

1 1/4 cups	milk	300 mL
1/2 cup	maple syrup	125 mL
2	egg yolks	2
2 tbsp	cornstarch	25 mL
2	peaches, pears or bananas, peeled and sliced	2

1. In a small saucepan, whisk together milk, maple syrup, egg yolks and cornstarch until smooth; cook over medium-low heat, whisking constantly, for 2 to 4 minutes or until boiling and thickened.

2. Arrange fruit in 4 individual serving dishes; pour hot custard over. Cover and refrigerate for 1 hour or until cool.

Per serving	
Calories	201
Protein	4 g
Carbohydrates	39 g
Dietary Fiber	1 g
Fat - Total	4 g
Saturated Fat	1.5 g
Calcium	110 mg

INDEX

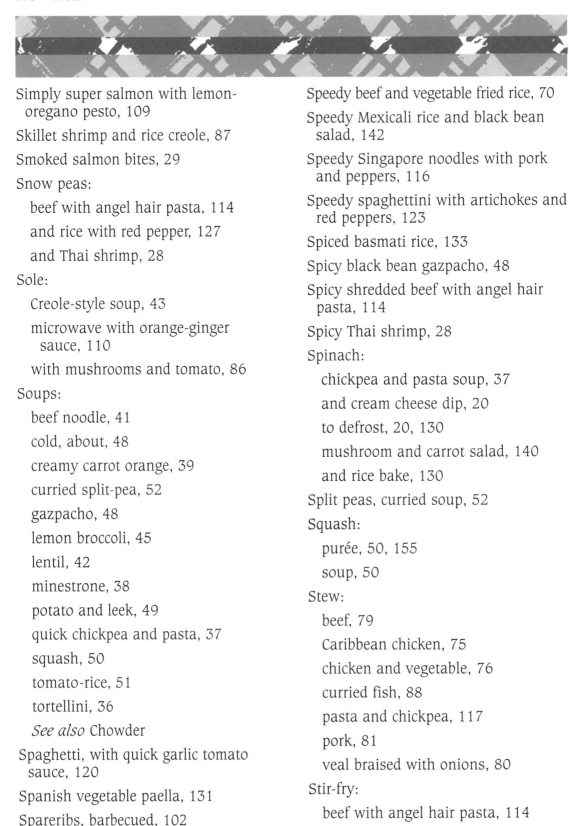